FROM HARVARD TO
HOMELESS: JOURNEYS OF
A MILLENNIAL NOMAD

# FROM HARVARD TO HOMELESS:

## JOURNEYS OF A MILLENNIAL NOMAD

FRANKLIN SOOHO LEE

NEW DEGREE PRESS

COPYRIGHT © 2021 FRANKLIN SOOHO LEE

All rights reserved.

FROM HARVARD TO HOMELESS:
*Journeys of a Millennial Nomad*

| ISBN | 978-1-63730-684-0 | *Paperback* |
| | 978-1-63730-774-8 | *Kindle Ebook* |
| | 979-8-88504-032-7 | *Ebook* |

*To Patrick. You're a trip. Thank goodness I love you.*

*"I love those who can smile in trouble, who can gather strength from distress, and grow brave by reflection."*—*Leonardo da Vinci*

# Contents

| | | |
|---|---|---|
| DEDICATION | | 5 |
| EPIGRAPH | | 7 |
| INTRODUCTION | | 9 |
| | | |
| **PART 1.** | **TO BE GAY** | **21** |
| CHAPTER 1. | COMING OUT | 23 |
| CHAPTER 2. | LOVE IN THE TIME OF CORONA | 41 |
| | | |
| **PART 2.** | **FROM HARVARD TO HOMELESS** | **65** |
| CHAPTER 3. | THE H-BOMB | 67 |
| CHAPTER 4. | DEFINING HOMELESSNESS | 85 |
| | | |
| **PART 3.** | **FREEDOM AND LIBERTY FOR ALL!** | **97** |
| CHAPTER 5. | PAVING MY ROAD | 99 |
| CHAPTER 6. | BON VOYAGE! | 119 |
| | | |
| ACKNOWLEDGMENTS | | 129 |
| APPENDIX | | 131 |

# Introduction

---

Imagine your world is turning upside down. You are at risk of losing your job; you got an unexpected hospital bill; you encounter a pandemic. The last couple of years have been a reminder to the world that our worst nightmares can come true.

Being as anxious as I am, I decided to take a big risk in my life—perhaps more drastic than other risks. I decided to pursue "vanlife." Vanlife, like it sounds, is a lifestyle characterized by living in a van. For some, vanlife is picturesque, promising Instagram-worthy photos. For others like myself, the lifestyle was a necessity.

Naive and inexperienced, I planned and executed vanlife with numerous challenges.

Luckily, the big risk came with big rewards. Vanlife jumpstarted my interest in socioeconomic issues, alternative housing options, and financial security. Vanlife also provided me with an immense sense of freedom. Perhaps, most importantly, it led me to love—but more on that later.

On Friday, March 13, 2020, when my workplace notified workers that we were expected to work remotely due to the worldwide pandemic, I was ready. As I was nearing ten months into vanlife at that point, I drove from Washington, DC, to New Jersey. For a couple of months, I stayed in Airbnbs to experience farm life in Virginia. Soon after, I drove to California to see my sister. On the road, I found my partner, Patrick, who had relocated with me from Indiana to Maryland.

As you can imagine, most of my friends and coworkers (and myself) have had trouble keeping track of my journey, which makes this book all the more valuable to me. Knowing now that the only constant in life is change, I hope that the snapshot of my yearlong commitment to vanlife will always remind me of the freedom I experienced. These memories, no doubt, will also drive me to work harder for a brighter and more secure future.

While there are many challenges to pursuing vanlife, I have found the lifestyle, especially as a millennial, to be freeing. To be specific, the idea that a young professional can pay 30 percent or less on housing is immediately appealing.

Millennials face a different reality than baby boomers or Gen Xers—one being lack of financial freedom. While millennials are arguably the most educated generation, we are also swimming in student loan debt. In fact, CNBC reported in November 2019 that millennials earn 20 percent less than baby boomers did at the same age in spite of being better educated. I am not all too surprised considering that, unlike my parents who never attended college let alone graduate school, I had to take out $100K in student loans before getting both my Harvard and Georgetown degrees.

According to Josh Bersin in a *Forbes* article from October 2018, while wage prices have increased over the years, they have not increased with the rate of inflation. What is more is that the percentage that an average millennial spends on housing is substantially higher than previous generations, as shared by Jacob Passy on *MarketWatch* in March 2018.

Ultimately, living inside your vehicle may be a viable option to get ahead in life for both yourself and your community. Take for instance Shawn Pleasant, a 52-year-old who was once a high school valedictorian and who chose to go to Yale even after getting into Harvard (unlike me, who actually made the right choice) to study economics and eventually work on Wall Street. As reported by ABC7 in September 2019, Pleasant lived on the streets of Koreatown, Los Angeles—my hometown—for six years.

I can't help but wonder, what if Pleasant had a van? Could he, maybe, have had a more comfortable and pleasant experience?

I myself experienced a night on the streets of NYC back in May 2018. While I did not face ongoing homelessness, that night was a reality check for me in my situation. To me, it is no surprise that vanlife is becoming more popular in cities like LA, as explained by Andrew Collins on *Jalopnik* in July 2019.

Vanlife came into my life in the form of need. In the moment when I was walking through the streets of NYC without shelter, I realized that homelessness could, indeed, happen to anyone. Graduating from Harvard did not exempt me from life's challenges, as it shouldn't. Harvard, as an institution, signals privilege to many people—perhaps, for good reason. Harvard, in spite of their efforts to select a more diverse student body, still brings in half of their student population from families who are in the top 10 percent of the income distribution.

To be clear, I am thankful for my journey thus far. Thinking back, vanlife has opened my eyes to a new world. Over the years, I knew that I am not historically an outdoorsy person; I do not seek adventure. Perhaps it was due to my personality or maybe it was environmental, but I grew up risk averse, seeking comfort and security. Rather than committing to a passion, I considered what jobs might be available to me after graduating from college. I was not motivated by the ambition of getting a high-paying job or attaining prestige; rather, I hoped to find a comfortable job in which I could attain an ideal work-life balance. More immediately, I looked for a way to quickly attain financial independence from my family.

However, my life challenges have given me an opportunity to reinvent myself. I learned to navigate through the emotional complexities of life, although still not expertly; to recognize that not everyone, including my family members, could agree with me on every principle; and that, at times, I had to accept the unfair power dynamics of life. I studied hard and cultivated a passion for writing and policy research, not because I felt that it was a life calling, but I wanted to find a job that would help pay the bills. I pursued vanlife not because I was outdoorsy and adventurous but to find comfort and financial security in a world where I struggled to move from city to city for my education, a new gig and/or job, and maintaining (or severing) relationships. Through my life's challenges, I became interested in issues related to social injustice, free market principles, and housing policies.

Vanlife, for others, can come as a choice. Some of you may have first encountered the concept of vanlife as a lifestyle in your Instagram feed or through Youtube videos. Today, there are a plethora of Instagram feeds such as @project.vanlife that share the vanlife community at large. At the time I was writing this book, just looking through #vanlife, there were over seven million posts.

There are also YouTubers like Jennelle Eliana whose channel blew up in a matter of less than ten videos documenting her vanlife. Today, she has over two million subscribers, and I am a fan. I, personally, have found her videos refreshing; as a person of color, her vanlife story resonated more with me than many other Youtubers who happened to be white. The fact that she wants to have a farm someday makes her only more relatable and inspiring.

There are other people who have lived inside smaller vehicles. Katie Carney, who has more recently resorted back to living inside an apartment (like myself), impressed me by sharing her experiences living inside her car. Carney shows her experiences on her Youtube channel.

As you can imagine, living inside a smaller vehicle makes a big difference in your lifestyle—much like living in a mansion versus a studio. In fact, the differences are exacerbated since smaller cars have limitations in terms of installing AC/heaters, beds, sinks, and any other household items.

The point is that those who have pushed the boundaries are putting themselves out for the world to see. What we need to realize is that this transparency is powerful. It has the potential to help people struggling to pay their monthly rent or student loan debt to consider other options that may put them on a road toward financial stability.

Living inside your vehicle—whether it be a car, a bus, or a van—is appealing because it offers an alternative, or a combination of need and choice. It gives room for us to turn the concept of housing, shelter, and lifestyle on its head. In this frame of mind, I strongly believe that there are ways to make living inside a vehicle a reality for others who have less room to take risks or make sacrifices. While I genuinely believe that this could be anyone, I specifically consider LGBTQ+ minors and young millennials and Gen Zers entering into the workplace as people who could benefit from more affordable housing options that are mobile and—in general—more flexible.

Imagine that our cities suddenly open safe parking lots to any type of vehicle. Imagine creating a similar space that is both insulated and temperature controlled, with restrooms and showers and perhaps with Wi-Fi access and a communal kitchen. In some ways, I imagine these parking lots are working spaces like the notorious WeWork that rented out rooms to companies that did not have permanent physical locations for a large number of employees. Providing parking spaces as work spaces, I think, is an interesting concept as workers are becoming more individualized and mobilized and markets are headed toward individual entrepreneurs who need to be nimble and constantly adapting to a new world.

The concept of such spaces in a city is not entirely far-fetched. In cities in Japan, there are tiny rooms that come in the form of capsule hotels. It is my belief that many more people can benefit if we can create safe havens for people who live inside their vehicles who wish to easily settle down in new cities.

Living inside your vehicle today comes with a unique set of challenges. For one, there are worries over law enforcement. While it was not technically illegal to live inside your van, neighbors might report you regardless: what would you do if you saw a suspicious-looking van parked in your neighborhood, and you suspected that somebody was inside? There are other policies that outlawed nudity in public spaces meaning that people changing inside their cars could have trouble if they did not have the proper layout to remain discreet. There are also issues of creating a driver's license without a permanent address, not to mention issues of safety and security. These are and continue to be issues that I deal with as a vanlifer.

That said, safe parking lots are already a reality in California, catering to the unsheltered homeless living inside their vehicles. A February 2019 article from the *Bloomberg CityLab* found that unsheltered homelessness is growing. Luckily, safe parking programs from San Diego to King County have been providing some of these homeless drivers a safe place to sleep during the night. With the first official launch of a safe parking lot in Santa Barbara in 2004, there are now safe parking lots in San Diego and Los Angeles. Safe parking lots, while having challenges of their own such as securing consistent funding from the government and accepting only a handful of applicants for their limited parking space, are proving to be in high demand. Data suggests that in Los Angeles alone, there are three thousand unsheltered homeless people living inside their vehicles. While safe parking lots cannot accommodate everyone living inside their cars, they show great promise to some who are looking for a stepping stone to get their life back on track.

Now, in a similar vein, imagine safe parking lots throughout the United States. Imagine safe parking lots with temperature-controlled car homes in Boston, NYC, or DC that also provide security measures and legal compliance. Such lots have the potential to provide millennial and Generation Z individuals with the ability to ease into internships and entry-level jobs in a way that high rent and moving costs cannot. These factors discourage young people from losing all their hard-earned money to the high cost of living.

Ironically, as a vanlifer, I started 2020 with the resolution to *hold my ground.* In the popular Aesop fable of the father, son, and donkey heading to the market, the father is continuously swayed by the opinion of others, eventually killing his own donkey before having the opportunity to sell it in the market.

Today, I feel that the valuable lesson of "please all, and you will please none," is ever so paramount as we are undergoing dramatic challenges: natural disasters, pandemics, demographic changes, and economic instability, just to name a few. In a chaotic world full of divisive tweets and polarized news, the pursuit of truth is essential to pave a road toward a brighter future.

The payback, so far, has been immense. In researching the struggles of exploring affordable housing options like vanlife, I have found it interesting to forecast societal changes that might occur if more people opted for mobile home options. Furthermore, what I found more interesting—especially as a policy researcher—was how people of color, people from lower financial means, and people who might have trouble navigating through the legality related to getting a driver's license, dealing with street parking enforcement, and other activities related to living inside your vehicle might be severely disadvantaged to even consider a more reasonable housing option. In discussing my findings, I hope that I contribute toward a society that is more freeing, extricating people from financial, geographical, and psychological constraints. By illuminating the issues at hand, I believe that the discussion can shed light on the problem more clearly and help us find a solution to create a more equitable society.

With that, I am excited to share my journey with my readers. To ensure that readers can best navigate my book, my story is divided into three sections.

Part I covers how my sexuality pushed me toward vanlife and its outcomes.

Part II explores the various privileges and handicaps in our society, mostly as a way to think about the issue more critically. The juxtaposition in the title, *From Harvard to Homeless*, is intentional. As a Harvard student, I recognize that I hold life privileges that others dream of. At the same time, we should recognize that, while all struggles are relative, a prestigious degree does not exempt a person from the possibility of homelessness. This is applicable to those who may be wealthy currently but have faced uncertainty due to the pandemic. The point is that nobody is safe and that our society can benefit from more empathy and compassion.

Part III summarizes both my vanlife and personal journey.

I started vanlife with the fear of being honest. I felt that there might be those who saw my pursuit itself as failure, as there might be stigma against someone who is unable to find a conventional form of housing. I felt that there were those who would be offended by my book title, *From Harvard to Homeless*, as they might think I was choosing a catchy title simply for book sales. Other times, I felt nervous about putting my life on paper at the risk of exposing parts of my story that I was not entirely sure how the audience would perceive, let alone know if everything I had decided to do was entirely legal (such as getting a UPS address to make my driver's license). Overall, I continue to write today knowing that there is still a part of me that fears judgment. I realized that as much as I wished to appeal to everyone, I could not appease everyone around me, from my parents to my colleagues, my friends, and my network. In an honest reflection of my needs, I could finally choose freedom.

Ultimately, this book is about freedom—the freedom to live a healthy life, the freedom to live a happy life, the freedom to share my story honestly.

Bon voyage!

# PART 1

# TO BE GAY

# CHAPTER ONE

# Coming Out

---

*"The most common way people give up their power is by thinking they don't have any."*

—ALICE WALKER

Back in May 2018, to avoid spending a night with my mother who had disowned me previously for coming out as gay, I spent a night homeless in the streets of NYC trying to find a shelter to house me. She and my sister had booked a plane ticket to chat with me without reserving accommodation, and I felt uncomfortable with the thought that they would spend any more minutes with me—albeit in a way that I disapproved of. I told them that I would be staying over at my friend's place, as I had been too embarrassed to admit my situation to anyone and was not confident that I would be able to find a place to spend the night.

At first, I thought it would be easy to simply Bing the nearest shelter that would house me. I should have known better because, that night, I wandered through the quiet sidewalks scavenging for a park bench to sleep on. It was a moment of realization that no matter how much I prided myself in working through various hardships in life, there were those who were undergoing deeper struggles than myself. After all, that night, I had a job to keep me afloat and even the cash to get a room if I was really desperate. The thought, however, that I would have to break into my dwindling bank account when I was only five months into my first job was scary, and I decided to persist a bit longer out on the street.

Earlier that year, six months out of graduate school and about to start my first full-time job in about two weeks, I came out to my parents by phone. Amid all the shouting and crying going back and forth, they told me that I had one of two choices: I would rescind my job offer and return back to LA to start therapy, or they would disown me.

At that moment, I decided on freedom rather than security. With a dwindling bank account that might only last me for two months in NYC, I decided to take my chances on starting my career. The two hellish weeks that followed are somewhat of a blur. All I remember is chugging bottles of wine to lull myself to sleep every night, otherwise I would get nightmares. I, someone who had been so careful about drinking too much even during my college years, could not bear to see my reality. I felt that I had no future and that I was living day to day—waiting for my new job to soon distract me from my emotional grief.

Today, I realize that my story is not unique. Data from the *National Estimates* (2017) show that one in ten American young adults ages 18–25 experienced unaccompanied homelessness at least once during the last twelve months, with one in thirty for adolescent minors ages 13–17. A disproportionate number of these individuals are members of the LGBTQ+ community. In fact, LGBTQ+ youth have a 120 percent higher risk of being homeless than heterosexual youth, according to a brief prepared by the University of Chicago.

TedX speaker and LGBTQ+ activist Melissa Moore shares that 40 percent of homeless youth are LGBTQ+ youth. I consider my story fortunate. I was not a youth at the time I came out to my parents, although I grew up with the constant fear and risk. As Melissa shares, "When you're young, you're gay, and homeless, you just disappear." Keeping that in mind, I sometimes think that, as someone with parents that had expressed their views throughout my childhood, I am both thankful for my upbringing. While I would have preferred to have parents that were understanding of my sexuality, I also felt that their clear signal helped me elongate my time to attain the resources I needed for freedom.

Essentially, as I was just a bit older, a bit more educated, a bit further in my career, I did not disappear like other youth. To me, these numbers are heartbreaking, because I genuinely believe that I would not have been able to figure out a way to move forward if I came out to my parents prior to getting my first job offer. That said, my narrative is not limited to LGBTQ+ youth.

In reality, homelessness can happen to anyone, and it is often not a choice, as some might like to assume. Take for instance Jack, who became disabled after getting slammed by a truck, or Jennifer, a single mom who suddenly could not pay rent after losing her two jobs. These are only two stories in which there are about twenty in the nonprofit Invisible People's website. The point of these stories is to highlight that there are hundreds, thousands, perhaps millions throughout the world that "blame homelessness on the person experiencing it instead of the increasing shortage of affordable housing, lack of employment, a living wage or the countless reasons that put a person at risk." Many people may be about to experience this reality with the ongoing coronavirus pandemic, as unemployment rates are at an all-time high, meaning that people are more vulnerable than they may have been previously.

I am aware that many people find it easy to blame the victim. On a car ride together, I remember one family friend sharing, "It's a shame; only if they got a job," while looking out at homeless people in the streets of Koreatown, Los Angeles. While I do not remember the context in which those words were spoken nor where the car ride was toward, I do remember feeling conflicted by the statement. My parents, too, had grown a life out of poverty. I was not confident that I could lead a much better life myself. While I agreed that everyone is ultimately responsible for their own livelihoods, I felt that I was much closer to the state of the homeless people outside considering that I was living under my parents' roof knowing that I was, in their eyes, breaking the rules by being gay.

Even in the present day, looking at the world around me, I sometimes have trouble identifying a specific skill or talent or a particular reason why someone would hire me. While I am thankful for my job, my education, and my current livelihood, the impostor syndrome is intensely real for me sometimes.

Stories like Shawn Pleasants', a Yale graduate who started experiencing homelessness in his mid-forties for six years, make it harder for me to think that I would one day become exempt. In my eyes, Pleasants had every reason to believe that he would be exempt from a life of homelessness, as he showed great promise as a Yale graduate who studied economics, worked on Wall Street, and started his own business throughout his lifetime. While our education may statistically help us increase our earning power, it does not guarantee a life immune from homelessness. Ultimately, it is important to read through Pleasants' story with empathy and understand that success does not necessarily come to those who worked hard. At any moment, all your hard work can, in fact, be swept away since nobody is immune from the world's challenges, and the risks persist no matter how much we lower the chances.

Among these challenges, one factor seems to stand out: poverty, not having the money to rent or buy a place to live. The issue of poverty is complex—especially in understanding how our society has criminalized poverty in the past. According to a *New York Times* article from February 1972, Fred Graham explains that the US Supreme Court case *Papachristou v. City of Jacksonville* ruled a vagrancy ordinance in Jacksonville, FL, as unconstitutionally vague meaning that "it was unconstitutional to punish persons as vagrants under vague laws that outlawed such conduct as loafing, 'nightwalking,' and avoiding work." In other words, the court's ruling suggested that the homeless cannot be penalized for sleeping on public property when adequate shelter is not available elsewhere.

What is important to note in this decision is that consideration of vagrancy laws is relevant to the racial profiling we find in our policing system today. Racial profiling is closely tied with our bias in associating socioeconomic background with skin color. In this way, when the Supreme Court found it unconstitutional to criminalize being poor—or appearing poor—it gave weight to the idea that the policy could not retain unlimited discretion, as explained by Risa Golubboff in an article from *Time*. The article, "The Forgotten Law That Gave Police Nearly Unlimited Power," reads, "The officer on the beat in the 1950s and 1960s saw such threats everywhere, in the 'queer,' the 'Commie,' the 'uppity' black man, the 'scruffy' young white one…When he walked the streets questioning and arresting the scum, the flamboyant, the detritus, and the apostate, he brought vagrancy laws with him, and he did his job." The ruling from *Papachristou v. City of Jacksonville* not only approached the issue of homelessness from empathy but as a critique against a racist and judgmental society that victimized and penalized people based on their being rather than their actions.

Unfortunately, the rulings from 1972 did not stop the continued injustice in our society in the last decade. National Public Radio shared data in March 2014 that showed that people of color are continuously criminalized at higher rates, and as much as luck matters, being poor does not help those who have been victimized by the system to rebound from their disadvantages. For one, failing to pay court fees itself, regardless of the crime—big or small—is considered a crime in our system that could elongate one's sentence for months and years. Imagine having to spend three days in jail for catching a fish out of season or, worse, spend a year in jail for stealing $2 worth of beer.

In reading through such injustice, it is important to recognize the system failures. While some may tout that "rules are rules" and that failing to pay for a fine is a crime, the reality is that our court system is not designed based on justice but on banking from citizens by laying out a spider web—targeting those who are easiest to victimize first. As Peter Edelman, author of *Not a Crime to be Poor*, explains, "It doesn't matter—it's just about money," and "People of color pay the highest price." What's more, "courts require people to pay what they are alleged to owe even before they can get a hearing on their guilt or innocence and their ability to pay."

Although—with the privilege of being Asian American—I grew up away from the criminal justice system, much of the narrative resonated with me since a young age. Growing up, my mother regularly lectured me on the reality of our criminal system, which, thinking back, was an effective way of keeping my discontents—the verbal and minor physical abuse at home—private. In my mind, I could tell that it was easier to abide by the rules of the house (keeping inside the closet among other things) than deal with child services protecting minors from abusive parents.

Although my environment at home might not have been ideal, I knew that having a permanent housing address, a school to attend with free breakfast and lunch, and the knowledge that my parents expected me to graduate high school and possibly even attend college like my sister sounded like a good deal compared to a system that could not guarantee anything. Ultimately, I did not want to be a statistic.

Recently, as it relates to not being a statistic, the title of a *Vox* article hit me hard: "The hardest part about growing up poor was knowing I couldn't mess up. Not even once." Similar to

David Tran, I grew up with a delicate balance recognizing that I had a taste of privilege, and it gave me the feeling that I did not want to mess up my limited opportunities. "Being poor you cannot afford to fuck up the opportunity that comes along." With a smaller margin for error, I did what I could to follow a system that seemed to promise (almost guarantee) a bright future: get good grades, go to a respectable college, and find a well-paying job. Luckily, even with more socially conservative parents who could not accept a gay son, with lower expectations for grades, college, and job opportunities, I had some room to play around with my parents. I did not go hungry; I was not exposed to drugs; I could shower daily.

For many young Americans, it is probably a privilege to feel that there is a once-in-a-lifetime opportunity. With 20.1 percent of American households facing child poverty, according to *The New York Times* in 2016, many children do go hungry, growing up in chaotic environments with broken furniture, dirty dishes, and early exposure to drugs.

Throughout my childhood to the present day, I kept vigilant of my privilege because I feared that it might be taken away from me. I remained thankful and kept quiet about my struggle, recognizing that there are those who are less fortunate than I am. Sure, I was in the closet, but I was fed, I was educated, and I was content overall.

However, deep inside, I knew that the whole situation was a time bomb ready to explode. In my mind, much of the debate around climate change revolves around the same logic. Yes, we can continue to manufacture goods in the way that people enjoyed decades back, but it is bound to return in the form of hell.

Later that night, one of the more empathetic callers on the line told me that if I called tomorrow at an earlier time, they could reserve a bed to accommodate me. Every time I thought I had found a spot to sleep (since the weather was quite nice, it was not as challenging as it might have been otherwise) I found a reason why I could not sleep in the space. Whether it was because the concrete floor was too hard, there were other people sleeping that seemed to eye me suspiciously, or there was too much light for me to shut my eyes.

That night in NYC, as I finally found a quiet and discreet place to lay down for about two hours to sleep, I quickly recalled an article I had read as an undergraduate at Harvard regarding how some people had converted their family cars into homes. The article struck a chord with me as our family had struggled through the 2008 recession, and as a millennial, the struggles among the vehicle dwellers in the article who were trying to find work seemed deeply personal to me.

When I woke up to bird chirps around 5 a.m., I had an epiphany: I thought how much better my night might have been if I had a car to shelter inside. It helped that I recently had a conversation with Peter Glebo, a friend who had convinced me to go to NYC when I confided that I was not sure how to start my career after graduating with my master's degree from Georgetown. He had shared it would be a breeze for me to get a car loan if I wanted to. Peter, who had started his life in NYC right after graduating from high school, was a valuable friend and mentor that encouraged me to keep my hopes high as I navigated through a new stage in my life.

The whole idea of having a car seemed appealing…if I could make it work. Born and raised in Los Angeles, I had grown up with the notion that everyone had a car. While I consider myself a homebody, during my college years at Harvard, I also recognized the benefit of being able to afford a nice drive—especially during the annual moving season in which I would have to lug my furniture and boxes into summer storage. Above all was the thought that I could use car living as a vehicle to attain financial security. Prior to college, I knew that I could not rely on my parents for a stable life.

To me, my years at Harvard, from the very beginning, felt like an ephemeral dream. Growing up in a low-income household with parents who had never gone to college, I surprised my parents when they found out I had applied and—eventually—was accepted. However, what may be important to note is that my motivations were lopsided and arguably misguided as I was more attracted to the idea of attending a prestigious institution to expand my financial opportunities rather than academic achievement and curiosity.

As much as I enjoyed my classes for their intellectual rigor and meaningful discussions with professors and peers, there was a part of me that heavily hoped that my education would set me up for life—that I could escape what, I felt, was a restricted childhood due to financial constraints. I remember the many nights that my parents would work overnight, in overwhelming stress, trying to make suit pants. As much as there was a part of me that resented my parents for being unable to provide some of my needs and wants, as I compared my life to my friends at school, I also recognized that my father had learned his trade in his forties—never having graduated from even elementary school and eventually picking up any jobs available throughout his youth. He had long-standing health issues from his early years, and they were reminders why I should appreciate the opportunities I had been blessed with.

And so, when given the opportunity to work, I did. During my college years, I worked for a student grill and a temp agency and regularly browsed study labs providing small compensation for participating in their research. Ironically, like many immigrant families, I was also shaped by the "American dream" suggesting that working hard, which meant that focusing on my studies as a student, promised a bright future. Anxiety over both education and money was constant. It is, perhaps, the reason why I decided to pursue a master's at Georgetown after completing my bachelor's at Harvard. According to Elena Ramos's article, "Nearly Three-Quarters of Harvard Grads Pursue For-Profit Jobs in 2018," 83 percent of students decide to continue graduate or professional school to continue discovering what they are interested in. I felt that I was not prepared to join the workforce—especially as a first-generation college graduate from a low-income household.

To be clear, Harvard is stellar in providing opportunities to their students regardless of their background. In fact, as shared on Harvard's official website, Harvard College places emphasis on providing for low-income students—with 20 percent of Harvard families paying nothing to attend—while making an effort to select students from a wide range of backgrounds, albeit Harvard still selects many students from wealthy families. The problem, however, as shared in Max

Larkin's 2018 article on *wbur,* is the fact that Harvard brings in students from a wide range of backgrounds does not guarantee that the student body will integrate in an organic and healthy manner—just like having different racial and cultural groups in American cities does not mean that racism and prejudice do not exist. I remember the occasional calls with my sister during college talking about how some students never experience having to file for financial aid or how I once heard that a student did not have to apply for any summer scholarships for internships or study abroad programs because they already had internships lined up for the next three years. Again, these were not really complaints per say, considering that I was in a position of privilege to even apply for such opportunities, but just a recognition that there were a wide array of experiences within the student body.

Recognizing the delicate balance between privilege and need, I eventually turned to vanlife as I thought it was the most sensible choice to live a dynamic life where I could live my youth without eventually regretting not taking a chance. It was a way to challenge social norms that had an unusual bias against the poor. It was a way to recognize the enormous strides we made, as a society, toward lowering poverty rates worldwide. It was a way to recognize that our actions matter. Empathy matters. A genuine and accurate understanding of our society is the foundation to create a better society.

What's more, I felt that vanlife could offer other Americans— perhaps other students from immigrant families struggling to find independence and mobility—a new way to pave a road toward a brighter future. To some, now with the forced stagnation from the pandemic, Americans may seem to have been traveling all too much previously. However, data shared from an article in *Axios* shows the contrary: Americans are moving less, specifically moving less to relocate for new opportunities. Numbers reveal that since the 1950s, young Americans relocate half as much as before—surprising considering that traveling costs are arguably cheaper with more technology today than half a century ago. The most concerning part of the data is that young Americans are most likely immobile because our society is less mobile economically, meaning that young adults are trapped in their jobs and their environment.

To be clear, my discussion around American immobility is not related to travel for pleasure—frivolous and possibly damaging to the environment. My discussion around mobility relates to the disappearing American dream. Millennials are more likely to stay in place today considering the high rent price of cities and limited guarantee of job opportunities. Young Americans are delaying marriages and childbearing due to financial pressures. Ultimately, immobility hinders freedom and the ability to maneuver chaining individuals to their homes.

If my parents had been accepting of my sexuality, I probably would have continued on my life in a similar trajectory. In May 2018, it hurt my pride that—at the age of 25—I still had to rely on my family to find an apartment that I could live in. When my mother and sister flew into NYC from LA, I felt vulnerable knowing that they could chase me to my permanent residence at a whim's notice. I wondered how I might find the independence and freedom that I had craved throughout my childhood. Thinking through these thoughts,

I continued to struggle to find a place to sleep, homeless shelters and all. I spent the rest of the night walking from sidewalk to sidewalk; I even tried sleeping inside a playground. The thoughts from that night became my life calling.

Around the break of dawn of my homeless night in NYC, I went to my office, as I was working at a social service agency as a paralegal at the time, and saw two young men, looking tidy and composed, who told me that they were kicked out of their homeless shelters because they had missed their curfew after working overtime at their workplace. My brief encounter with these two men did a couple things for me: while I had already suspected, I once again realized that they again broke the stereotype that a homeless person would look disheveled, malnourished, and problematic; there were systemic problems in government assistance programs for homeless people and they could not be assumed to be reliable forms of housing; and economic opportunity is an important factor in discussing alternative housing options.

Looking back, my concerns and my decisions were real and part of a larger narrative; a college education is important for millennials' earning power. Data from the Pew Research Center reveals that earnings of young adults have only increased slightly for the college educated compared to older generations, while earnings decreased for those only with some or no college experience. Unfortunately, in spite of the growing number of educated millennials, we have less accumulated wealth than previous generations due to the late start in our economic careers since the 2008 recession. This may help explain why, even as I graduated with a higher degree, there was a level of concern in joining the job market.

I am reminded of the early days when my sister lamented, "It's a Catch-22, they want to hire people with years of full-time experience for an introductory position."

I still remember the immense amount of pressure and stress of looking for my first full-time position. As a first-generation college student without any family members who had gone through an official job hunt after graduating, I was overwhelmed by the process. I continuously read through my emails, social media feeds, Google searches, internship websites, anything that might open a lead. Ultimately, I found the most promising lead through a Facebook post on a Harvard alumni page for an opening as a paralegal. As expected, my network, the privilege that I was fortunate to seize, helped me land on my feet.

Since then, many things have changed, and I consider myself fortunate. Although I have over $100K of student education loans as I am writing this book, I feel lucky to have landed a dream job as well as a passion project. What's more, I am certain that my education has empowered me with the tools to move forward knowing that I am capable of overcoming the obstacles ahead of me. This is not to say that things are easy. In the last couple of years, I remember lying down in bed calculating how long it would take to pay off my debt, considering how much more I could pay off each month. Considering the date shared on Annie Nova's 2018 article on CNBC sharing "facts about public service loan forgiveness," I wondered if I might end up being within the 0.85 percent of applications who completed the Public Service Loan Forgiveness (PSLF) after ten years of public service work. Ultimately, I decided that I could not assume that any one way would work out and that I should cast my net just a bit wider. I could not assume that I would ever be able to pay off my loans, let alone ever return. I came to the conclusion of carpe diem: to live my life to the fullest minute by minute. I needed to align my long-term goals (to pay off my student loans, find my passion work, etc.) with daily actions that would give me fulfillment rather than hope to start after I had resolved all my ongoing challenges.

From the very start, I realized that the journey would be difficult. I had never bought my own car; I had never driven on a highway. Vanlife was a serious challenge considering I had little experience driving, camping, and adventure-seeking in general. In fact, I remember the struggle of passing my driving test on my fourth try as it was the last obstacle to get to Harvard. I asked my parents if I could apply for a government ID instead of a driver's license; I felt it was too difficult and unnecessary. It was, fortunately, close but no cigar; I either passed my driving test to get a license or I rescinded my college acceptance because I could not board a plane with a valid government ID. Anyways, the following months after deciding to pursue vanlife were a roller coaster with immense highs and lows. I made a goal to start living inside my van by the end of October since that was the month my apartment lease would end. At the time, I had no idea how to purchase a car, where to park my vehicle, nor how to find the space and money to renovate my new living space.

Along the way, luckily, I slowly shared my plans with close friends and a coworker hoping to keep my project discreet and found enormous generosity in terms of knowledge and resources ranging from the ideal street parking right outside my workplace, a trustworthy mentor to guide me during my first drive through the highway, and a woodworking shop that provided me with the labor and materials for the renovations pro bono. Meanwhile, I struggled with new challenges: getting my car loan denied, jumping from Airbnbs to sublets, and getting persuaded to write a book with a potentially controversial title: *From Harvard to Homeless*.

I share all of these struggles because they highlight how much support an individual needs to plan and pursue vanlife. It is not as easy as making your bed one morning or deciding to cook a special meal. As such, it is my goal to make vanlife and other alternative housing options easier for others. While vanlife may never be as easy as completing a daily chore, my hope is that it may be easier than getting an apartment in NYC or DC or LA or Boston.

I write all this recognizing that there are plenty of efforts at the local level to make alternative housing options available to the public. For example, an article from *Megaphone* from November 2019 reported that a charity Beddown, in Brisbane Australia, decided to have a pop-up in which they would use empty parking lots as homeless shelters during the evenings. Meanwhile, as explained by Dan Fitzpatrick from a December 2019 article in the *Tiny Home Industry Association*, California—facing the pressures of the rising homeless population—is making various efforts to explore alternative housing options ranging from tiny home villages, backyard housing, and movable tiny homes!

In writing this book, I decided to come out—not because I felt that it was important to publicly announce my sexuality (which I realize can be an empowering act) but because the vulnerability gave me the courage to pursue what I felt was right for my life. I came into vanlife expecting to live in the shadows, thinking that being homeless was wrong and that my lifestyle was inherently criminal.

Luckily, with the resources and support around me, I realized that this may not be the case. In understanding how policies are made, I realize that our communities create societal rules for people to live and, hopefully, thrive! To create a more just and equitable world, I am convinced that we must cultivate options for vanlife, tiny homes, and other alternative housing options so that people can adapt and evolve according to the new world ahead.

## CHAPTER TWO

# Love in the Time of Corona

---

**MILLENNIAL DATING CHALLENGES**

"¿Tienes una novia?" One of the workers helping renovate my van, pro bono, asked me in Spanish, which, by the way, means, "do you have a girlfriend?" Reading my previous chapter, surely you can imagine what thoughts ran through my head.

Somewhat flustered, I said, "no." In that moment, knowing that I was seen as heterosexual and seeing how perceptions may change based on my answer, I tried not to discuss the issue in more detail.

Being good-natured, he joked, "there is enough space in this van for a wife and a child!"

I laughed. It was all in good fun.

That said, I started my journey with the vision of remaining single. After all, data in the current world suggests that being single is the norm. Data from 2019 by the Pew Research Center found that compared to Gen Xers (53 percent), boomers (61 percent), and "silents" (81 percent), only 44 percent of millennials were married at a comparable age. In addition, data show that Americans are more likely to live alone compared to anywhere else in the world.

With dating getting substantially harder in the United States every year, I sought a life to find community rather than a lifelong partner. While I did come out, I did not do so to pursue a partner. In fact, thinking how unrealistic it may be for me to find a partner, I had made plans to live a happy life for the rest of my life being single.

Life has a tendency to throw you curveballs.

With the start of the pandemic in March 2020, I started my life on the road. At first, I made my way into New Jersey to stay with a friend; then, I moved to a farm in Virginia; soon after, I headed toward San Diego. With growing screen time for both work and entertainment, I also experimented with dating apps—something that I avoided initially in fear of ruining relationships within a near geographic proximity.

With the pandemic, I found myself being more adventurous online. I had known a number of my friends who met their long-term partners on dating apps. In fact, not too long ago, I attended a wedding between two people who had met on Coffee Meets Bagel. This is not too surprising considering the Pew Research Center found from the 30 percent of

Americans who have used a dating website or app, 12 percent have been successful in finding a committed relationship or even, marriage.

When I found myself at a rest stop in Indiana, I chatted with guys on Grindr as a way to cool off from the long drive. I had to get some rest for the long trip ahead. What followed were some sweet messages from one guy, which piqued my interest. Thinking that I would unlikely go on another road trip, I decided to take a chance and meet Patrick, my current partner of one year.

What followed was an interesting experience. I remember we started our time together in Patrick's apartment in Richmond, Indiana—still with dirty dishes, bad lighting, and the stench of cigarettes. With a crowded table, Patrick slowly adjusted his room to fulfill my needs for an office space.

Upon learning about his life story, I realized that our journey together was integral to writing this book. Many of his stories have changed the trajectory of this book, especially as I transitioned from vanlife back to an apartment near my office in Washington, DC, albeit with many life upgrades. In the same way that my vanlife helped me discover Patrick and a new chapter of my life, it is my hope that our story may help you discover new chapters of your life.

**GEOGRAPHIC MOBILITY**
As mentioned, with Patrick as a new life partner, I soon transitioned from vanlife back into renting a beautiful studio near Washington, DC. As it did for most people around the globe,

"love in the time of corona" brought about many changes in my life. In my mind, there is no doubt that my van contributed to a smoother transition.

For instance, vanlife allowed us to move from one apartment to another with minimal effort, as I could move all of our furniture and belongings in two trips. While we could not necessarily sleep in the back, as we were able to do during shorter excursions, we knew that we could move our lives with relative ease by sacrificing 8–9 hours of our time. In this sense, vanlife gives us freedom and peace of mind when we consider the current market volatility, job security, and overall unpredictable status of the globe.

Numbers suggest that the current world is less mobile; yet we also know that talented young adults prefer to move to urban areas, leaving others who could benefit from urban culture and education behind. That said, living through the experience with Patrick was eye opening.

Vanlife gave me the opportunity to introduce Patrick to NYC and DC at a fraction of the cost of traveling to both cities, especially as we paid great attention to following CDC guidelines for traveling with the ongoing pandemic. This helped immensely in getting a sense of how Patrick might adjust to a new geographic location and how we might make the move seamless.

Much of vanlife lowers the cost of mobility—geographically and psychologically. Eventually, as we both confirmed that we would like to move our lives to the DC, Maryland, Virginia (DMV) area, we were able to make the appropriate plans accounting for the possible risks and unexpected costs.

Seeing Patrick's failure to make it in Los Angeles, I sought to find a way to maximize our chance of success.

Unfortunately, Americans are less likely to be as mobile today. While there are various factors that contribute to this pattern, expensive city life, no doubt, contributes to the general difficulty in moving geographically. Unfortunately, this reality not only makes it more difficult for rural Americans to move over time, it likely spirals them toward less opportunities to ever find mobility and, more importantly, freedom.

Some may argue that geographic mobility is a choice. Patrick's and my experience, however, proves otherwise. While conversing with Patrick, I learned that he spent five years in Los Angeles homeless. In hopes of escaping the small city of Richmond, Indiana, he left for the big city after chatting with a stranger on Facebook. With the promise of a romantic relationship and the shelter to start his new life in the city, Patrick realized that he had been "catfished" only after he made the move.

Patrick's following struggles, as he continued to dream of making his life in the new city, proved that while he could survive in Los Angeles, he could not lift himself out of poverty. Living off of his Social Security Disability Income (SSDI), Patrick also pursued penny art to make extra cash. Eventually, as Patrick struggled to make ends meet in Los Angeles, he had to return to his family in Indiana for support. Patrick explains that he felt that he was imprisoned in Richmond, Indiana, forever—at least, until he met me.

Unfortunately for me, for a while, I felt imprisoned by Patrick—mostly from the fumes of cigarettes in his apartment.

Patrick started smoking at the age of twelve, which means that he had smoked for over twenty years. With the cigarette smoke seeping into my newly long pandemic hair, I convinced him to switch to vaping. Now that he has converted to a cessation device, Patrick is working toward decreasing his nicotine intake and eventually quitting altogether. Knowing that his father had to remove a large portion of his jaw after throat cancer, he wishes to quit as quickly and safely as possible.

## DRUG ADDICTION

The issue of nicotine addiction—more largely, drug addiction—is important in discussing my relationship with Patrick and vanlife at large since it relates to both our financial struggles and geographic dependence.

There is no doubt that Patrick's vaping habit has taken a toll on our finances, especially as our expenses went up after moving into a studio near Washington, DC.

Patrick has also noticed that with fewer smokers in DC, there is a societal pressure to stop smoking and vaping. Unfortunately, with a habit that has developed over twenty years, Patrick realizes that the environmental pressure (although helpful) is not quite enough.

Data support Patrick's observation with the Department of Homeland Security's and Centers for Disease Control and Prevention's finding that smokers "living in rural areas are more likely to smoke 15 or more cigarettes per day than smokers living in urban areas."

Patrick is somewhat fortunate that nicotine is not only widely available throughout the United States but also legal. Although high tax spikes are in place to curb sales, Patrick is still able to reduce his cravings and think of quitting strategies gradually.

Meanwhile, there are still many drugs that are illegal, and as many drug addicts are criminalized, they experience a downward spiral in which they are unlikely to ever recover.

One of the deadliest phenomena of this reality is the opioid epidemic, in which more that ninety Americans are dying every day from overdose! What is more, data show that rural America is struggling with the opioid epidemic most intensely.

For many Americans, drug addiction is not a choice. While some have the willpower to overcome any obstacle, we must accept that many are likely to succumb to the many deadly attractions in our daily lives, starting with social media that has the ability to quietly and effectively eat up our most precious asset: time.

**EDUCATION**

While Patrick had a troubled history starting with his nicotine addiction followed by his years of homelessness, I retained hope that our relationship would work out because of his strong desire to continue his education. During our time together, I learned that Patrick had previously attempted to get his GED. As I drove him to the Richmond Adult Education Center, we learned that Patrick could not only prepare for the GED exam for free, but his exam fee would also be covered with some additional funding that the center had received due to the pandemic.

Having accumulated nearly $100,000 in student debt knowing that it does not guarantee a high-paying job, I do not blindly advocate for universal college education. Instead, I believe that our nation can enhance our K–12 education system by incorporating more practical skills into our curriculum (such as tax preparation, personal financing, registering to vote, etc.) and having value in the system itself.

Regardless, seeing Patrick taking actions toward improving his life, I know that education, in one shape or another, is ultimately the most important factor in equipping the public to improve their livelihood.

It is no surprise that with a more educated world, the amount of competition for traditional jobs has increased. That said, as will be explored further in chapter five where I discuss the new frontier of cybersecurity jobs and how they are especially appealing to millennial nomads, there is much room for work in new fields. Vanlife allowed Patrick and I to explore a new realm together, as we navigated through a dynamic world.

Part of education are skills like driving and overcoming government bureaucracies. Patrick, having various disabilities, had a limited knowledge of social cues. As such, at one point, Patrick had been written up by a Social Security Office so that he could never again visit the office physically in person. This was devastating considering that Patrick lacked the additional support he needed to get through the nuances of government bureaucracies.

Luckily, I had my fair share of working for a social service agency and frequently going to the DMV to help Patrick bypass many of his struggles. Starting from teaching him how to navigate his SSDI website and strategizing the time and date of phone calls, Patrick realized that he could more easily attain the help he needed.

Soon enough, I helped Patrick get his driver's license. The required course was expensive, and getting a car for his driving exam was a nightmare—once again proving the level of privilege to get educated for useful life skills.

Car rental shops like Enterprise would not rent out their cars to a driver with only their learner's permit. With my van being oversized and there being no way to see through a back window, my car would not qualify for his road test. The fact that DMV reservations had to be reserved months in advance did not help due to social distancing measures from the pandemic.

Fortunately, Patrick was lucky. The driving instructor kindly accommodated our request to rent out her car, even going as far as being Patrick's chaperone for the road test since it was during my work hours.

There is room to be hopeful as virtual classes mean that people living in underprivileged areas have the hope of getting a top-quality education—if they have access to quality Wi-Fi.

This is all to say that getting one's driver's license is a process, something that is difficult to achieve without support. Luckily, Patrick passed his test on his first drive (unlike me who had to take the written test a second time to finally pass the road test on my fourth try). It was interesting to hear later that the road test evaluator had inquired why Patrick had never gotten his license. For me, a license was necessary to get on a domestic flight to college, as I had no other government ID that I could use. My high school ID would no longer work when I turned 18. In a sense, my privileged upbringing (still growing up in a low-income, first-generation household) had already put me a lot ahead in considering alternative housing options that Patrick never got to consider before meeting me.

Another privilege may simply be in knowing how to properly identify or reconfigure your vehicle. For example, I received one parking ticket in the past for parking my vehicle in an area where commercial vehicles were not allowed. Confused, I later learned that while I had actually registered my vehicle as a personal vehicle, it was still considered commercial to the ticket officers, as my vehicle did not have a window behind the driver's seat. In learning about this regulation (which to this day I don't know how I would have had to know beforehand, as nobody in the DMV had shared the information with me) I had to rely on the kind workers from Bespoke of Winchester to place a porthole window on my van.

**CREDIT SCORE**
When I met Patrick, I soon learned that he had no credit score. With a $500 phone charge that Patrick felt he was wrongfully charged for, Patrick had a blank slate. In retrospect, now knowing Patrick's spending patterns and financial history, I believe that this was a blessing in disguise. While I was already in a tough financial journey with my

student loans, Patrick could start off with a clear conscience. I felt that my knowledge and Patrick's blank slate put us in a positive position.

Through experience, I had already learned the importance of good credit. Back in September 2018, soon after deciding to pursue vanlife, my car loan was disapproved. Ironically, with a credit score of "very good," my car loan had been disapproved with a red mark on my report due to a small Harvard loan that I did not realize I was not paying. It was devastating news knowing that the loan amount was a mere $900 compared to the nearly $100,000 loan that I had accumulated at Georgetown for my master's degree. In retrospect, that, too, was a blessing in disguise as I would have started my payments much later than three months past.

Amid many life changes starting from a new job, coming out to my parents, and transitioning to a new life in New York City, I admit that I wasn't monitoring my credit closely. It is important to note that I was in the process of starting my payments through six different loan streams making the entire process more complicated. Additionally, my Harvard email was disabled once I went to graduate school in DC. I moved to NYC for work and did not realize that there was mail that had never been delivered to my permanent address until it was too late. Suspecting spam calls and voicemail, I also failed to suspect that I had not been making Harvard loan payments.

In spite of these difficulties, many may continue to think that I was irresponsible for failing to pay my Harvard loan those three months. They are right; ultimately, I am responsible for my mistakes. That said, financial oblivion may be more common than you think.

Fortunately, when people take active steps to improve their credit score, they can be repaired and improved more quickly than one might think. Soon after resuming the Harvard loan payments, I was able to get my car loan for my current van—about six months later.

Today, I have paid off my Harvard loan payment in full! While the red mark is still on my credit score report (and will likely continue to last for another four out of seven years), the mark has not impacted me negatively during my apartment search and credit card spending increases, among other important things that credit scores are used for (although, I am expected to briefly explain what happened in a call during my credit score checks). I suspect that I will have no problem getting a mortgage loan if I choose to purchase a home. Having enjoyed vanlife so much, it is unlikely that will happen anytime soon (although, never say never)!

Additionally, Patrick and I are in a good position, as I have helped him navigate through similar financial hurdles. After paying off his outstanding phone bill, I have encouraged him to get a credit builder card. At the time of writing this book, his score is "fair," which will likely improve in the upcoming months and years. If Patrick chooses to get a student loan during his time in college, my experience will likely serve as a lesson for us both in navigating through the difficult financial world successfully. For the time being, Patrick dreams of getting a car of his own, perhaps an electric sprinter van that we can renovate to travel together and pursue vanlife full time.

## HEALTHCARE

Speaking of credit scores and finances, like many Americans, Patrick has struggled with healthcare coverage. Although my struggles have been nowhere near Patrick's, I have also had a number of challenges with my health that shake my financial stability.

Unfortunately, a healthy body (including teeth and vision) is not guaranteed, even if they appeared perfectly healthy a few months before.

Although I had known that my gums had been receding in previous years, they felt especially sensitive recently. In November 2020, I was officially diagnosed with periodontal disease at a critical/aggressive state. The dentists explained that my condition was permanent and that the bacteria in my gums—while they could be controlled and monitored—would never go away completely. As they explained about the antibiotic, Arestin, they suggested that I go on with an oral procedure in which I had to get a medical loan of $2500 dollars through CareCredit. I decided to get the recommended treatment, knowing that letting my teeth and gums worsen would only lead to more pain and likely more expensive procedures in the future.

Seeing how expensive the procedure was, I asked the dentists if they could advise me on getting a better dental plan for the future. Taking a look at my company insurance, they assured me that I had one of the best coverages and that the loan I had to pull out was standard for such procedures.

The most frustrating part of the experience was the fact that I had been doing everything I could to maintain healthy teeth. I made sure to brush twice a day, flossed, and rinsed my mouth with mouthwash two to three times a week. I have had no cavities since I became a teenager. During childhood, I had some traumatic healthcare experiences due to bad teeth—and poor health—ever since my eyesight quickly deteriorated during my early years.

One of my childhood traumas growing up was when my third grade teacher told my mother to get my eyes checked for glasses. Once the eye doctor confirmed that I would have to get special prescription glasses, I remember my mother looking glum at the expensive price tag for my new lenses. Since my sister did not have to get glasses until she was in high school (and even then her glasses were much cheaper since her eyesight was still relatively good), I felt a pang of guilt, especially when my mother expressed her frustration with the cost of the varifocal lenses which were more expensive than the bifocal lenses that my sister and my mother used. Unlike my sister and mother who would mostly use their glasses to supplement them for reading, I would have to wear them daily for all activities.

When I take my glasses off for sleep, I occasionally have terrible nightmares of losing all my teeth or losing sight when I'm terribly stressed. The dreams are so vivid that I usually walk to the bathroom to check my teeth in the mirror. Perhaps due to this trauma, some of my dentists noticed that I ground my teeth at night. Knowing that it doesn't necessarily look the most attractive, I put on a mouth guard each night; and fearing that another bacterial infection might again recede my gums, I use denture cleaners to wash it weekly.

In spite of all these challenges with my vision and dental history, I consider myself fortunate. As a young and healthy male in my twenties, I have been fortunate in that I have rarely had to go to the hospital; in the rare instances I went for a check-up, I was told that I was healthy.

On the other hand, I have spent a lot of time with Patrick to: (1) identify his health conditions and (2) find affordable treatment options with his limited finances and insurance.

This has been more than challenging, as Patrick has had to pull out a couple teeth due to cavities. Before Patrick met me, he did not make the habit of brushing twice daily or even once a day. As you may imagine, this did not sit well with me, especially as I got my gum procedures. Noticing that he still had healthy gums, I made an effort to remind him again and again to brush twice *every day*.

More importantly, Patrick has been hospitalized for Crohn's disease, which has interfered with my work schedule and deadlines.

Lastly, which I think may be the most important, Patrick has struggled to find therapists for his mental health.

For most of his life, Patrick did not realize that he had Asperger's until his half-sister noticed symptoms and suggested that he find a doctor to get checked.

Amid the move to the Washington, DC, area, hospitalization for a Crohn's flare-up, and visits to a dentist, Patrick has been racking up health bills left and right. What's more, unlike in California or Indiana, Maryland's Medicare coverage has been garnishing up to nearly 20 percent of his disability check.

There is a commonly shared saying: it is often cheaper to be rich and expensive to be poor. This has certainly been the case for Patrick.

Currently, Patrick is stressed with an issue that he probably never had to think about before. Almost on a weekly basis, I follow up on Medicare and Medicaid coverage, as I constantly think of ways that we can get the dental services he needs. However, there is really no simple way to go about the issue, as Patrick not only has no Medicaid after moving to Maryland but has no credit to apply for coverage. Although I have researched some cheaper services in universities, the reality is that even those amounts are proving difficult considering the amount of savings that I have broken into to cover his learner's permit, driving school fees, and college fees, among the various other financial challenges that come with moving forward in life (such as moving to a new city).

As we continue through the financial journey to become cheaper, but richer, I realize that the federal government does have some role in providing structural changes. For Patrick, his saving grace may be his SSDI, a monthly allowance that can help him as he adjusts his life to resemble a working professional, as well as his educational grants (noting that his financial aid can always be compromised if he is unable to keep up with his schooling, an overwhelming fear for somebody who has not been in school for nearly twenty years). With sixty months of income guaranteed to transition into a career, there is room to maneuver through life's challenges without having to be tied down to a career. In short, there is still room to experiment with job preferences, which is important.

It should be no surprise that a healthy population means money saved for the government, as healthy workers and consumers are the foundation for a healthy economy. Yet, Patrick's healthcare (as well as my own) has proven to be challenging.

Yet, as Patrick has mostly recovered after his colonoscopy and my gums now look pink and healthy, we continue to feel grateful and move forward with our lives. The best we can do is to practice healthy habits while continuing to advocate for better healthcare for all.

**WHAT IT COSTS TO BREATHE AIR**
In discussing Patrick's challenges, I am simply making the point of how difficult it is to survive as a millennial in today's world without support from family. While societal progress has helped us attain more security, technology, and material goods at a cheaper cost, the price to simply exist has gone up.

In hyperbolic form, it costs an arm and a leg to simply breathe air in our society.

When Patrick first expressed his interest in taking our relationship further, he wooed me with the prospect of helping renovate my van. In retrospect, I was foolish, and he was sweet. Ultimately, considering how it worked out, I have no doubt that it was for the best.

Patrick had experience helping his father with home renovation work.

In his twenties, Patrick had left Indiana in hopes of finding new opportunities but could not find a way to sustain himself in an expensive city. He faced many issues that may seem small but that can have grave consequences in the long term. He came back to his hometown feeling anxious. At that time, and presently as well, Patrick received Social Security Disability assistance.

It is important to note here that with numerous government and local regulations, homeless shelters have stringent rules that make it difficult for people to get housing. While it is my strong belief that the government should always aim to support our citizens, I also believe that—as our time and resources are oftentimes limited to being better trained and equipped to be effective watchdogs—the government needs to understand and provide individuals with the freedom to choose the housing and shelter they desperately need.

It may be helpful to bear in mind that in the years after coming out to my parents, I approached life differently. I was much more fearless, thinking that I no longer had to cling so desperately to living a "good," "proper" life. When choosing vanlife, I came with the thought that I was willing to accept death if it came to it. Reading an article about a man/woman who had died inside their car in Florida (and people did not know about it until much later), I laid in bed many nights thinking about whether I would wake up the next morning. Although I did not fear death itself, the thought of somebody finding a rotting corpse inside a random vehicle felt less than ideal. If there is an afterlife or reincarnation, I would prefer that good karma follow me around.

To retain some good karma by avoiding a situation in which a random stranger would have to discover my corpse inside a vehicle that was about to get towed, I started confiding in some close friends who might contact the police if they could not reach me. This is around the time that I strongly felt that if more people started to live inside their cars, it was important for local as well as state and national laws to support rather than penalize people living inside their cars. In the same argument in which the poor are penalized for being poor and that it is more expensive to be poor, the poor were stripped from shelter when they needed it most.

From the short but intense yearlong vanlife experience, Patrick and I have much to look forward to as we continue moving onward in this journey. We have moved into an apartment nearby my office, and we are slowly planning to get back on the road when we are ready. I have purchased a cellular signal booster to upgrade the van, as I have found limited Wi-Fi an enormous detriment in pursuing a nomadic lifestyle.

In discussing all of the successes and challenges in pursuing love in the time of corona, I must point out that vanlife gave me an opportunity to meet Patrick in the first place. In this sense, Patrick is the perfect opportunity to show how directly vanlife can change the life of individuals who are less privileged than myself.

I have taken note of my experiment with vanlife in the past year, and I am undergoing/planning a number of upgrades.

We have made some upgrades to the van, as we have traveled together to NYC, DC, and Louisville, KY, ranging from a headlamp in the driving area to replacing the windshield wipers. Patrick, having experience with handiwork, is planning to help make some additional adjustments to the van based on my experience with the space.

From the beginning, I saw vanlife as a powerful tool to better lives, especially for the most vulnerable. The year 2020, if anything, has reinforced my views. Vanlife, if provided with the right support, can help young adults adjust to a dynamic environment where we are trying to make sense of the numerous global challenges ranging from climate change, healthcare, housing prices, and general economic volatility. It is my hope that my ongoing experiments and struggles may provide valuable insight into possible solutions.

**BACK TO THE BASICS**
Whether it comes to shopping for groceries, having professional clothes, or even entertainment to fill our days, the way Patrick and I structure our lives is different. While I consider my life more sustainable than Patrick's, it is also true that I find it hard to judge his routine too harshly, as I had my share of struggles changing my habits while adhering to my parents' more traditional values.

While there are no right answers to how one should live life, I have found Patrick's daily routines to be unsustainable—sometimes his fault and other times not so much. Over time, I have reminded Patrick: until he finds a way to continue his education and eventually find a job, his security blanket is nearly nonexistent. Together, we both struggle, knowing that we can do things to make our lives better.

In a way, our love in the time of corona has allowed us to build a relationship that could have never worked out in any other scenario.

There is no doubt that the current state of the world has been an anomaly with the pandemic, and we are one of the byproducts of the changed world. Additionally, the pandemic has added complexity to our development, as we expect the upcoming post-pandemic world. Patrick and I have slowly eased into the public eye, a natural and helpful transition to me as I have been coming out to the public as well

The power to dream is powerful. A video highlighting the possible difference between Homo Sapiens and Neanderthals suggest that one of the few advantages that Homo Sapiens may have had was in our imagination. Our ability to think beyond what is immediately visible gives us incredible strength.

Our creativity has allowed our relationship to be mutually beneficial, a symbiotic experience. Now that the passenger seat was occupied, Patrick attained the role of DJ and occasional GPS navigator. He could also look through the car compartments while I drove. Seeing the utility of his aid, I went and installed an interior light and a battery-operated light switch in the back room. Instead of a sleeping bag and a small mosquito tent, we opted for a two-person camping mattress.

In the upcoming months and years, Patrick and I will likely hit many more milestones. I am sure that each one will continue to build on our relationship, which will ultimately pave a road for a more exciting and happier future.

Potential is a powerful motivator. Vanlife and Patrick are both forms of such potential. Potential has the ability to reimagine a future in a world where we can foresee the imminent dooms from climate change, economic uncertainties, and nuclear proliferation. The fundamental challenge of the way we live—starting from where we sleep to how we use the restroom—fundamentally alter the future of humankind, hopefully in a positive way.

When I started my vanlife journey, it was an ambitious project, and I persevered because I saw the value of what it might become. Knowing the potential to create a better future for a new generation, who might be undergoing the same struggles that I was going through, was a motivating force.

Thinking back, vanlife provided me with the opportunity to see relationships differently. With the ability to move from city to city and knowing that I could physically meet up with people after chatting through an app first, I had increased my chances of meeting a possible partner.

For some, Patrick's struggle comes off as a downer. To others, I am sure that I appear to be someone with many flaws. Together, however, we see each other's strengths. In Patrick's GED graduation, I found one of the speeches regarding value insightful in illustrating this point.

In the graduation for his GED, one of the speakers shared a story about value, which resonated with me. In the story, the father instructed his daughter to get a price check for his old car from three different dealers. In the end, after one dealer priced it at $1,000 and the other at $500, the last priced it at a whopping $100K, as he was an antique car collector who understood the price of the Nissan he was purchasing.

Much of our value is subject to the eye of the beholder. Yet, recognizing that there are many eyes to consider in this world, we should focus on those who truly value us for who we are. More importantly, in moments when we feel underappreciated, we should learn to appreciate ourselves. In concluding her speech, she asked all the graduates to pick up a mirror and tell themselves, "Gosh, you are good looking! I have so much potential."

Seeking validation is a natural tendency, but putting your trust in others stems from a lack of trust in yourself. Vanlife and my experiences with Patrick have put many obstacles in my way—all learning experiences, showing me how capable I really am. Today, I am learning to love who I am, building better confidence and trust in myself. I believe this is a journey we all can relate to, Patrick included.

With vanlife, I was looking for financial freedom, and en route I found love. May we all take the journey to be proud of who we are, to be happy and perhaps, gay.

# PART 2

# FROM HARVARD TO HOMELESS

## CHAPTER THREE

# The H-Bomb

---

**WHAT IS THE "H-BOMB?"**

In the early Facebook days, I jokingly put up a post on my bio: "I am the "modest-*est*" in the world. Time to time, I still grin at the smart aleck post; I am still quite proud of thinking of it. As a Korean American, I felt that Korean traditions and culture pressured people to be humble when they desperately wanted to stand out and be recognized for their excellence. As such, I felt that there was a subculture to brag about how modest one could be.

This paradox, I realize, is universal. Attending Harvard, I learned and quickly mastered the H-Bomb dialogue.

"What is the H-Bomb?" you might ask.

The H-Bomb refers to students who make a concerted effort to avoid sharing that they are attending "Harvard" so as not to appear pretentious or arrogant. This often means that a Harvard (or MIT) student will likely say that they "go to a school near Boston/Cambridge," rather than the college itself.

My conversation around the H-Bomb is relevant to how social media has been romanticizing vanlife in recent years. To some, avoiding the H-Bomb is a genuine strategy to avoid bringing unwanted attention, while to others it is a form of humblebragging. Similarly, for some, vanlife is a survival strategy, while for others it is a glamorized lifestyle that allows for Instagram-worthy photos. It is at this point that I would like to clarify that I am guilty of utilizing the H-Bomb for both strategic purposes: at times to avoid attention and, at other times, to draw attention.

Similarly, I have incorporated vanlife into my lifestyle as a survival strategy as well as an icebreaker for cocktail parties. I firmly believe that the act of humblebragging or the vain practice of sharing selfies is not inherently wrong. There is value in sharing our academic and/or financial achievements; at times, for influencers or companies, it is a job. Yet, our present culture discourages an honest conversation in favor of name-dropping and trauma porn, which makes it difficult for us to make decisions that are truly good for ourselves, whether it be for our pocketbooks or for our morality. As a result, in a society that focuses so much on advertising and marketing, we do not spend enough time considering whether name-dropping or utilizing shock marketing tactics such as trauma porn are truly unethical or problematic.

With that, I would like to spend this chapter discussing my thoughts on name-dropping and trauma porn, among other relevant topics related to our value and egos. I believe that this would be especially helpful to those who are interested in pursuing alternative housing options as they gain popularity—ranging from tiny homes, vanlife, and skoolies (more on this later in Chapter 5: Paving My Road").

With constant name-dropping and addictive trauma porn over the years, we have grown accustomed to the relentless advertisements from our favorite YouTube stars to podcasters. Meanwhile, fashion retailers and even grocery stores utilize sneaky tactics to encourage customers to buy their products by placing them strategically in their stores. The thought that companies and individuals have ulterior motives—to sell and profit in our capitalist society—can rub people the wrong way. It can feel slimy and inherently wrong. Growing up, my parents gave me the impression that rich and wealthy people were inherently immoral.

Today, I know that my parents are not the only ones. We can see the evil caricatures of rich capitalists in our media ranging from Scrooge or even the mixed media coverage of ex–Amazon CEO, Jeff Bezos. Over the years, we also see the other end of the spectrum, as we see stars whose job is to appear vain (Kim Kardashian, hint, hint). In my position, it is difficult to make a judgment that one is better than the other. However, to make the assumption that all advertisement and marketing tactics are immoral is deeply problematic. Before we criticize Jeff Bezos and Kim Kardashian, we should also recognize that marketing strategies around climate change or LGBTQ+ rights, while not perfect, do progress our discussion around difficult issues.

Furthermore, utilizing marketing and advertisement can be an effective way to change social perceptions in a positive way such as increasing acceptance and diversity, reducing bullying, and rebranding "nerds" and "geeks" as "cool," among others. Recently, I have been interested in the topic of minimalism, as I believe that our society is ready for a rebranding of the concept so that it may be more accessible to the public.

Previously, minimalism often involved a certain aesthetic, a color palette, and key words, whether it be in the form of a writing, image, or video. However, a number of influencers and writers have been challenging this thought, as minimalism is being seen as an approach to becoming more intentional with our belongings and learning to truly appreciate the items we have and care for.

Today, I view vanlife through the same lens. Vanlife, for me, was an approach to resolve problems that I think are commonplace among millennials: having to struggle through student loans, job opportunities, and high housing costs in cities.

With that, I also want to touch briefly on the issue of trauma porn. For those who are not well versed, trauma porn refers to utilizing or showcasing a group's pain and trauma as a marketing tactic, whether it be to donate money to Africa by showing photos of malnourished children or showing images of landfills to discourage unsustainable consumption. Trauma porn has the potential to be highly manipulative and deceiving, as corporations often utilize it for profit rather than for truly altruistic purposes. In that sense, trauma porn is immoral.

That said, I recognize that there are elements of trauma porn in my "coming out" story. It is, however, intentional. My story is genuine but also strategic so that I may deliver my message clearly and effectively. I do not feel that I, nor anyone else for that matter, should feel pressured to apologize for sharing my authentic self to the universe. I hope that my next story regarding my decision to attend Harvard over Yale may help clarify what I mean.

## HARVARD VS. YALE: FINDING MY IDENTITY

I still remember refreshing my iPod touch on my walk back home from school relying on public Wi-Fi as I awaited the college decision for Harvard. Having gotten into Yale early, I secretly thought that I might also have a chance to get into Harvard. I suspected correctly, as I trembled reading my acceptance email (which was confusing since it did not start with the typical "congratulations" message that most colleges use in acceptance letters).

Anyways, I like to share my experience in choosing to go to Harvard over Yale because I feel that it does a good job in discussing a first-world problem (to keep our spirits up) as a way to build a tool that I can use for more serious topics.

Not too long after I got accepted to Yale early, I remember an enormous amount of pressure to choose Yale over Harvard. My dream school had always been Princeton. When I did not get in, I was drawn to Harvard.

When I shared my decision to attend Harvard, I remember one person commenting on my Facebook post—albeit respectfully—asking why I had chosen Harvard over Yale. From the people who brought Gilmore Girls to the fact that

Anderson Cooper had attended Yale, I felt a pressure to choose Yale over Harvard simply because there was a sense that Harvard was overrated.

I am proud of myself for sticking to my gut decision, as I now feel confident that it was the right choice. While Harvard and Yale are both amazing schools and I realize the genuine curiosity that others had about my decision, it was ultimately the better fit for me.

Harvard opened up many doors, and it would be a lie to say that I do not realize the many privileges I now have. That said, with nobody in my network who had gone to Harvard, I started my college life unprepared. I have had to constantly make up my educational and resource gap creatively. The struggles helped me grow, but the intense pressure has led to life burnout.

The reason why my decision to attend Harvard over Yale is important is because it speaks to the tricky decisions that came afterward and continued to disrupt my thoughts every day, even now. I was extremely lucky in that I was offered two great choices, and (to the outside observer) there was no wrong choice. At the same time, as I saw some of my colleagues choose small liberal arts colleges over Harvard—which I believe to be a legitimate choice for reasons ranging from financial to personal fit—I realized that gray nuances often confused my thought processes.

As a way to reset my decision making, I tend to return to the basics. My education has helped me understand that even the smartest and brightest cannot predict the future in its full accuracy; rather, we can use forecasting tools to try and direct our lives in the direction that we believe would make us happiest.

And in thinking of the basics, I have utilized the tools of stoicism and pessimism—learning gratitude from thinking of worse situations and outcomes as a way to plan ahead, always around impending disasters. With that I would like to introduce you to some of the most troubling events that triggered complex thoughts about privilege and tradition while I was at Harvard.

Wisdom gained as a result of attending Harvard then, eventually, from pursuing vanlife has challenged my preconceived notions of the world that I was living in again and again. Fittingly, this chapter is about privilege and tradition.

In a culture where we celebrate entrepreneurs and the American dream, I think there is an appeal of being the "cool" rebel in our society. In that sense, in the various cliques in my early school settings, I would describe myself as a "rebel against other rebels." As an Asian American, I fit into a stereotype: small framed, studious, and generally quiet. And yet, I quietly rebelled against the generalization of my identity, knowing that I was an individual with my own thoughts.

I remember my father calling my relatives to share that I had gotten an early acceptance from Yale. My father who had never graduated from any school including elementary school was so incredibly proud, except their response was contrary: "Where's Yale?"

When I finally got into Harvard, I asked if they knew where Harvard was, genuinely curious. My mother exclaimed, "Of course! Everyone knows where Harvard is!"

That reason, while it may be vain, has contributed to my college decision, and that truth, I now realize, is fine.

With the struggle of my first-world problems, I soon went to Harvard to deal with more serious issues ranging from cheating scandals, bomb threats, and identity fraud. While everything is relative in this world and there is more serious trauma porn that we can always delve into, I hope that the three examples I have gathered during my time at Harvard might serve useful for both myself and others who may be dealing with more serious issues.

## ELDO'S BOMB THREAT: WHEN PRESSURE TURNS TO DUST, NOT DIAMONDS

In 2013, Eldo Kim sent an anonymous email to Harvard University administrators claiming that bombs had been placed in two buildings on campus to avoid a final exam. As this was the same year of the Boston Marathon bombing, the incident brought about national press and concern.

To me, Eldo represents our natural human fear of failure taken to the extreme. In two contrasting op-eds in the *Harvard Political Review*, "We're All Eldo Kim," and "We're Not All Eldo Kim," two Harvard students write about how they personally relate to the intense pressure at Harvard, albeit in different ways. While one believes that Eldo's actions are understandable and the other believes that the action was too drastic and unacceptable, they both recognize the intense pressure among Harvard students.

That said, I asked: is this pressure limited to Harvard?

The answer is no. We find that pressure exists everywhere. It is an ongoing fight that will never end.

In starting vanlife, I was nervous that I would not be able to pull through. I was worried about judgment. At the same time, I felt that homelessness was a possibility and I had to find every competitive edge to get ahead in life.

At work, I started my job with little to no experience, and I had imposter syndrome.

Ultimately, I can relate to some of the desperation that Eldo might have felt. While I can in no way support or legitimize his actions, there is a certain level of empathy in understanding the frustration he may have felt from external pressures. As one article from *The Harvard Crimson* reported soon after the incident, "Students interviewed…were not surprised to hear that the suspect is a student, citing Harvard's highly stressful environment."

Continuing the thread of some Harvard jargon, there is the notion that Harvard students often live inside a bubble.

The "Harvard bubble," refers to the fact that the Harvard campus, while close to Boston, is distinctly separate in the city of Cambridge and that students tend to stay inside the vicinity rather than venture out.

While the Harvard bubble can refer to the geographic nature of the campus, it also refers to a state of mind in which students are accustomed to Harvard's distinct culture, often losing sight of the bigger community.

One of the arguably most psychologically detrimental aspects of the Harvard bubble is the intense pressure for students to be successful in both their academic and social lives. Living through the experience, I intensely felt the pressure to both "study and party hard." Motivated by the desire to break the stereotype of being a bookworm, Harvard students took their extracurriculars seriously, if not more seriously than their academics.

Having experienced the pressure of the Harvard bubble, I could see how other students might find themselves taking chances that they might not have taken in other settings. I see Eldo Kim's bomb threat as a possible scenario that likely happened as a result of the intense pressure of the Harvard bubble.

A feeling of desperation is created from our brain's response to our environment. While our society does a great job framing our expectations, we start to create rules that are unsustainable.

That said, I also appreciate bubbles; they are shelters. At times, shelters help us focus and grow until we are ready to deal with life outside.

**ABOUT ABE LIU AND IMPOSTER SYNDROME**
During my freshman year, I remember fighting through imposter syndrome. Like many others, I had presented my best self in my college application, and I suddenly felt that the college had fallen for an impressive façade.

Perhaps if I had listed a couple of my less impressive AP scores, if I had a different teacher write up my letter of recommendation, if I didn't so easily score a perfect score on the SAT II Korean exam, would Harvard have accepted me? After all, my dream school, Princeton, had rejected me.

More importantly, I felt that I had a mask on for such a long part of my life that I never had a chance to explore and find my authentic self. Knowing that my parents were critical of the LGBTQ+ community, I knew that they would not be supportive. I was used to keeping a face and hiding my identity. Amid these identity crises, I learned about Abe Liu.

Abe Liu was a 27-year-old who impersonated a freshman at Harvard, spending time socializing with other students, when, in fact, he was a student at the Harvard Extension School (HES). According to a *Harvard Crimson* article from December 2011, Liu explained that he had no mal-intent. He was simply lonely.

To a certain extent, I feel that much of our imposter syndrome comes from loneliness. During my time at Harvard, many assured me that imposter syndrome is normal and that we needed to remind ourselves that we deserved to be there. I found reassurance and continued on.

The trouble is that imposter syndrome can come in lethal doses when people take extreme measures to hide their authentic selves. Rather than accepting failure as a natural human experience, our society has continued to pressure us to be unrealistically successful based on an arbitrary gauge of what "success" is.

Not too long after learning about Liu, I also learned about Elizabeth Holmes, around the time that she was being covered for her ingenuity by giant finance publications like *Forbes*. There is no way to compare the level of atrocity in

Holmes's actions to Liu's actions, but it is a great example of someone taking extreme measures to appear as something they are not for personal gain.

As a society where we are starting our fights against disinformation and misinformation, it will be important to take a look at these issues closely—and not take them lightly. I feel lucky that I was able to observe these phenomena, and I do genuinely believe that these issues were felt more intensely because of the amount of pressure that comes from the Harvard brand. Students attend the university with added burdens and expectations, regardless of their prior mindsets. This is a matter of environment.

Studies show that our environment changes our mindset, actions, and rituals. In my mind, this is a natural Harvard phenomena that probably happens frequently throughout our society when we start to glamorize or romanticize small subsets that we idealize as the best. In this regard, there is a definite case for the thought that there is security in diversity.

In learning about Liu, I realized that my imposter syndrome, stemming from my insecurity about my identity, was unnecessary and unproductive. Finding my identity is important; constructing my identity can be dangerous. The thought that we delude ourselves to be somebody we aren't can be devastating—for both ourselves and the people around us.

### THE 2012 CHEATING SCANDAL: REEVALUATING THE RACE TO THE TOP

In discussing how a student could think to create a fake bomb threat to avoid a final exam or another creating a fake persona as a freshman at Harvard when he was not, the 2012 cheating scandal showed how pressure, imposter syndrome, and other factors could lead to problematic groupthink.

During the spring semester of my first year at Harvard, I learned that a group of students had cheated on an exam for one of the introductory government courses—a prerequisite for many students. While it was easy for me to point fingers in disdain, the event was traumatic in its own way.

Although I have never cheated on any exam while at Harvard, or on any standardized tests, I know that I do not have a clean slate when it comes to the many homework assignments, tests, and quizzes that I've had in my lifetime. For me, cheating is a societal issue as much as it is an ethical issue pinpointed to a single individual, especially considering that it could happen to a sizable group of students at a large and prestigious institution like Harvard.

As I share about the controversies of cheating, imposter syndrome, and societal pressures at Harvard, I want to stress that much of my observations are personal. They do not reflect the entire student body or the institution. That said, I feel that certain aspects of my thoughts may be universal, as expectations and societal pressures affect everyone.

What stood out to me, as I decided to attend Harvard after being rejected from Princeton, was the concept of grade inflation. "Grade inflation" was the idea that professors, for fear of getting lower ratings during the instructor evaluations at the end of the class, would be pressured to give higher grades so that students would be happier (and, therefore, more likely to give better evaluations). Additionally, as many Harvard students were likely to apply for fellowships, graduate school, and competitive jobs that might look at one's GPA, they would likely seek classes known to give better grades.

While Princeton was known to deflate grades, Harvard and Yale were known to inflate grades. In the actual setting where I interacted with professors from different departments and different classroom styles (ranging from group seminars, large lecture classes, and small classes), I felt that the practice was mixed. I could swear that some professors deflated grades simply to make the point that they were not inflating grades.

Regardless, the view that Harvard inflated its grade was a part of our reality. While some argued it was simply that Harvard students had more As than other colleges because they brought in more competitive students or others thought that professors gave out more As because they were more focused on their research and had their teaching assistants grade the assignments, those within the Harvard bubble and the ivory tower seemed to be constantly judging Harvard students' performance.

It is my belief that—within the framework of grade inflation, imposter syndrome, and intense academic pressure—the environment was ripe for students to join a problematic bandwagon. Humans are oftentimes unethical, not because they want to but because they believe that they have to be to be successful. There is a sense that if other people are doing it, they should do it too. Regardless of what one might say, I believe that we are all guilty. Consider climate change, a plight that does and will affect us all, and the amount of advocacy it requires to make a dent in our societal groupthink.

When we create an environment of intense competition without prioritizing the value of an individual, we are asking for disaster.

The concept of vanlife, for me, is a challenge to some of the societal norms that I believe to be problematic for our society. Why should we encourage larger homes and mansions when we know that it may unnecessarily increase the carbon footprint in our world?

Therefore, what is important is that vanlife and alternative housing solutions are continuously discussed and explored in a world where people are struggling with housing. While not all generations are in a position to challenge norms and defy traditions, the reality is that our generation has to rethink conventional knowledge (as we recognize that climate change and changing economies are the new normal).

## VERITAS: CHALLENGING "TRADITIONS"

As the oldest institution in the United States, Harvard is known for its many traditions. When I was a student, I was told that there was a checklist of things that Harvard students should complete before graduating, which ranged from primal scream to peeing on the Harvard statue.

Over time, what I have learned is that traditions are not steadfast rules. They change. What's more, at times, "traditions" are not traditions at all but simply peer pressure.

I was at Harvard at an interesting time (although this is simply my ego talking), considering that students were interested in antiestablishment topics, ranging from Occupy Harvard, divestment, and antihazing policies. Even the long established Finals Clubs were starting to disassemble during my time at Harvard, as they were pressured to either become co-ed or have their members be disqualified from fellowships and other opportunities once they graduated. There were some finals clubs at the time who, knowing that their membership was secret, resisted the change.

The truth here is that not all traditions have the same importance. While some traditions can and should stay, some are temporary constructions that should be readily let go. Take, for instance, the tradition of jumping from the Weeks Bridge into the Charles River. At first glance, it seems like an innocuous college tradition that requires a certain level of bravery and commitment. As suggested in *The Harvard Independent* by Hunter Ricards, such traditions are misleading and "impractical."

During my time at Harvard, I learned that primal scream was a recent invention. I also learned that diving off from a bridge to the Charles River could lead to death, especially under the influence of alcohol (a once-common practice during hazing rituals). Considering Harvard's long legacy, some were adamant in respecting traditions. However, what I learned was that while traditions are valuable, an erudite should continue to challenge previous thought through intellectual discussion considering historical context and the ongoing changes throughout the world.

A big part of this chapter is recognizing the big Truths and the smaller truths. This issue is important in our everyday lives, as we learn to distinguish the fights that we participate in and those we learn to accept and let go.

The concept is parsed out neatly in one blog post by *Doug in a Pub*:

*Truth with a capital T are the big Truths…. things that are not affected by viewpoint, experience or perspective—the easier of the two truths. Truth with a small t are the tricky ones, the ones that cause fights. The ones that lead to misunderstandings. The ones that are different for everybody. The ones that are completely shaped by perspective and our internal filters.*

In choosing the title *From Harvard to Homeless*, I had to go through the definition of "homelessness" and whether my experiences were truly of someone who had been homeless. As our understanding of the world changes, our smaller truths are allowed to change for the good of big Truths. In the example of the Harvard clock, John Quincy Adams, sixth president of the United States, enhanced previous time pieces as a way to measure time more precisely. Much of our traditions can also develop over time as a way to build a stronger Harvard community intended to create a more fruitful and fulfilling experience.

Recognizing that the concept of time is not the same as time found on a watch can have a practical purpose. Similarly, recognizing that "homelessness" may not literally mean having no "home" or, rather, "shelter" can be as problematic as it is useful. The concept of timekeeping has evolved over time, as it best helps society. At times, it comes in a calendar, sometimes a clock, sometimes in the form of numbers—as it is often displayed on our phone screens.

As such, the definition of homelessness needs to be considered in the context of societal needs. This discussion, as it relates to Harvard's veritas, is extended in the next chapter, "Defining Homelessness."

It is likely that Harvard will maintain much of its established jargons and quirks such as brain break, AB vs. BA, and concentration, but its most important quality will likely continue its long-lasting legacy: knowing when it's time to change and adapt. After all, the institution recognizes its Latin motto, "veritas," knowing that while "Truth" never changes, some "truths" change constantly.

CHAPTER FOUR

# Defining Homelessness

---

The issue of homelessness, ultimately, starts from our ability to maintain our homes. While my previous chapter dealt with the issue of privilege in one of the world's most prestigious colleges, this chapter extends that discussion of privilege to housing.

Vanlife, for me, was a euphemism for homelessness. It was a creative solution to cut my rent cost for something I felt was more tangible while earning myself mobility from the rigid bubble that my parents had wrapped me in. For some, vanlife is performative—an idyllic lifestyle, a self-expression of freedom and originality. With some vans costing more than a mansion or a luxury house, I can see how some people may view vanlife as vain and problematic.

That said, many creative minds who have tested and made the idea of vanlife more attractive (and then shared their knowledge with the public on forums like Youtube and blogs) have paved the road for novices like myself with limited resources. As such, it is my hope that my experiences may open up the minds of other people who, like myself, may have held negative prejudice against alternative housing options and rethink what it means to be homeless.

No matter your housing status presently, the reality today is that we are more likely paying more than in the past. While it may be no surprise that housing costs are skyrocketing, some may still find it difficult to believe that there is no state, county, or city in the nation today where a minimum-wage worker can afford a two-bedroom rental by working forty hours a week, as shared by CNN in July 2021. For those who consider a two-bedroom a luxury, the same worker can only find a one-bedroom rental in 7 percent of all US counties (218 out of over 3,000 nationwide). To this end, housing is an important issue for all minimum-wage workers in the United States simply because of the wage-to-rent ratio.

Much of our struggle to have shelter on a weekly or monthly basis, in itself, is a fight against homelessness. Vanlife, as it relates to easing or alleviating some of this stress, is a way to reconfigure the meaning of poverty.

Both my parents grew up in South Korea in extreme poverty. With General McArthur predicting that South Korea would not be able to resume back to their pre–Korean War economic levels until a century later, my parents vividly recounted the countless hungry nights throughout their childhood in addition to the general lack of resources that we take for granted in our lives today. One story that usually stroked my guilt involved my mother being punished at school because her parents could not afford to buy her art supplies to use in the classroom. As such, when I peered into the issue of privilege and homelessness, I always started my line of thought from, "things could be worse." In a way, it has been the source of my strength and success, as it helped me persevere through what I knew were lesser hardships (whether it be long nights writing my essays or working overtime for my part-time jobs during college and graduate school).

Yet, comparing struggles is not the best step forward. The fact that I do not have to face starvation does not mean that my struggle with student loans is not real. As we solve some of our more basic needs, it is only natural that we tackle larger problems. At our core, humans more or less follow the rules of three, as explained in a *Backcountry Chronicles* article, "Wilderness Survival Rules of 3—Air, Shelter, Water & Food:" (1) You can survive for three Minutes without air (oxygen) or in icy water; (2) You can survive for three Hours without shelter in a harsh environment (unless in icy water); (3) You can survive for three Days without water (if sheltered from a harsh environment); and (4) You can survive for three weeks without food (if you have water and shelter). For those of you who have managed to survive—including myself (lucky me!)—you are already luckier than most, especially considering that many of our ancestors lived through harsher conditions.

Considering this, defining homelessness might be more complicated than people think. For example, would somebody who lives in subsidized apartments or temporary shelters be considered homeless? "Of course!" some might say. Well, what about people who are living inside tents on the sidewalks you drive by every day? Then again, were you homeless on the night that you went camping? Ultimately, the answer to whether someone is homeless or not can be, to an extent, relative.

So, what is the definition of homelessness (I mean, officially)? According to Merriam-Webster, one of its many definitions, as is most relevant to the discussions in this book and chapter, is, "having no home or permanent place of residence."

This definition is too broad, especially in the policy world. For example, are soldiers or truck drivers who are expected to move every couple of years or weeks, considered homeless? What defines "a permanent place of residence?" The dialogue around homelessness starts from its ambiguous meaning with no definite place to start. The definition of homeless is long, convoluted, and changing—oftentimes contextual based on the circumstance of an individual or a family.

For instance, the definition of homelessness impacts individuals and families without full regard to their situation, probably as a matter of practicality rather than intent. The last changes in the definition of "homeless" by the US Department of Housing and Urban Development in 2012 added, "people who are living in a place not meant for human habitation," adding to a larger group of people experiencing homelessness. That is, until, creative problem solvers utilize the nuances to create new categories of housing that may be appropriate for the new world—a new generation of the most educated, open-minded, and talented individuals.

I distinctly remember how my mind shifted dramatically in the same apartment the day after my mother had visited NYC. On the day I returned back to my room after my homeless night, the apartment did not give me the same sense of happiness and safety I had felt. In other words, I was living in the same apartment before and after my mother's visit to my apartment in NYC, but my mental state had changed fundamentally, knowing that somebody could so easily intrude into my livelihood and personal space. Much of my decision to move into a van was a defense mechanism; my mindset was essentially in the framework of homelessness, as I knew that I was already struggling to pay for NYC's high rent prices. It did not help that I did not have full confidence at the time that my workplace would be accepting of sexual minorities, which kept me in the closet (although I now see that it was, in fact, a safe space).

I know that I am not alone, as *The New York Times* recently covered how LGBTQ+ youth struggle to find jobs even in a place like NYC, known for its cosmopolitan culture, due to perception. It is my strong belief that this mindset is what ultimately defines homelessness. The problem is that, due to the subjective nature of homelessness, it is hard for any organization (or even homeless individuals themselves) to recognize whether any person is truly homeless. Consider a study from the Hastings Center in 2013 showing that our cognitive functions change during times of poverty. The study showed that farmers, right after their harvest, made better economic decisions than before harvest, suggesting that people make better decisions when they feel wealthier (or when they feel that they are free from financial worry). In the same way that a farmer's brain capacity changed with the perception of how much harvest they had left, the idea of homelessness extends beyond whether a person has shelter at the instant moment to whether the shelter actually provides a sense of security to them.

In the past year, I have reflected on my mental state more often. As I've been navigating the world with my new partner,

Patrick, I began to see his and my past mental challenges more clearly; in some sense, the physical house is not as important as the sense of security that comes from other factors such as one's job and relationships. At the same time, some things did remain the same. I required shelter from the hot and cold nights, food to nourish me, and a way to look and feel presentable in the workplace. I have also felt this parallel in Patrick's diet of all places.

Despite the fact that Patrick has lived five years homeless, it does not change that he is unable to consume many of the foods that are provided in the food pantry due to Crohn's disease. Going through a typical educational or vocational program is challenging for him, regardless of his desire (and maybe even his commitment), due to his Asperger's. In my daily interactions with him, I constantly require feedback, as I experiment with the various life choices I can offer him ranging from whether he can consume celery or bell peppers so that his diet does not consist of only highly processed meats and carbs.

In that same way, vanlife provided me with some ways to meet my various needs in a different manner that was more palatable to me at the time. Yes, Patrick can force down peaches, but eating cherries could literally send him to the ER with hives. That said, Patrick also enjoys watermelon, cantaloupes, and granny smith apples. While I enjoy having a nice, clean space, it did not have to be particularly spacious or established. Rather, I preferred that it be mobile so that I could extend my freedom. Ironically, vanlife was a pursuit of comfort and financial security, which eventually led me to my life passion.

The reality today is that many young professionals, regardless of their academic pedigree, do not start off their career in the same way that previous generations had decades before. More millennials (and Gen Zers) rely on their parents as they go through college, internships, and starter jobs for their careers.

As an LGBTQ+ community member who knew that I could not rely on my parents for support, I found stability in lacking a permanent residence. Still, actively refusing myself a traditional form of housing came with a number of challenges—challenges that have initiated a lifelong interest in alternative housing.

Without proper plumbing, something as basic as using the toilet or brushing my teeth were especially difficult daily obstacles. *The New York Times* also shares the many difficulties having to find bathrooms to brush teeth or to find safe parking spaces considering that legislators are intentionally changing regulations to discourage people from living inside their cars—a cruel solution, which is only a temporary Band-Aid, a crutch to the problem.

Since the World Health Organization announced COVID-19 as a pandemic, the coronavirus has impacted the globe in more ways than one. Among them, I found the consistent media interest in our national and global economy fascinating – especially as we continue to push forward into the unknown. With the quarantine, our markets have entered into a historic recession with a historic high of claims for unemployment benefits. At the same time, the stock market is continually upbound leading to various economic speculations guessing the future impacts of the pandemic both short and long term.

While this uncertain time may be stressful for many people for various reasons, the biggest stressor, for me, has been my student loan debt. Whatever your stance may be related to the issue, the reality is that one in four Americans today have student loan debt with an average of about $30K. That said, I wanted to spend some time discussing the issue of student loan debt and its connection to my decision to pursue vanlife, especially as I, personally, have over $100K of student loan debt.

In a continued cycle of seizing more opportunities, I saw vanlife as my freedom ticket. I wanted the option to hedge in a world where my every decision seemed to have so much weight; the pressure that my actions would determine my future, my value, was overwhelming. As much as I had to make my college and graduate school choice knowing that I would be continually judged, I actively sought to find a way to reduce the pressure of securing a specific job in a certain city or state at a certain pay grade. Eventually, I sought to walk out of what I saw as a societal hamster wheel.

In walking out of the societal hamster wheel, I have found value in overcoming judgment from others – especially those preaching that you have a choice as a way to highlight your faults. While I recognize that people are quick to point at past mistakes and justify your failures (as well as successes), I have only recently been able to pluck enough courage to occasionally reassure myself that my decisions were, in fact, the best decisions I could make at the time.

That said, I am convinced that overcoming poverty, overcoming any financial obstacle, is difficult. Can we truly penalize people who are attempting to "get by" by living inside their cars or working overtime to get a bit more cash?

My story is vulnerable for a reason. It is my plea to society to recognize the underprivileged. While recognizing that I have more privilege than others for having a platform to write my story and share my narrative, I wish to highlight the struggle that many Americans are facing in our society today.

Requisites for getting a driver's license should, nationwide, change to include a primary address rather than a permanent residence address. This is discriminatory toward homeless or mobile individuals. It discriminates against people who are living with their family or friends temporarily, creating an already lopsided power dynamic. Rather than creating independent, healthy, and fully functioning citizens, we create slavish individuals who are continuously chained to a world of inequity.

The problem of having no permanent address or residential address is that you can't legally get a driver's license. This does not only impact vanlivers; it impacts homeless people who need homeless shelters to aid them. The problem is that homeless shelters often have troubles of their own.

What if you have issues with your family, significant other, or a stalker? What if you want to be able to move around freely?

In the years following, I remember my poor college summers lugging my storage boxes to the post office as I was unwilling to spend money on an Uber. Many times, I felt like crying in the middle of the street because I was so frustrated. It felt like such a waste having to move or throw out various furniture and items each time. It's been so liberating to know that I could start my new job in DC only a day after driving into the city! Vanlife in the city, for me, has been worth the trouble.

Being homeless never seemed like a far reality for me. During high school, I intended to find a part-time job to find a way to become financially independent. Nobody wanted to hire a minor, especially with no references. During college, I attended various career services, but my feeling was that all options I saw were incredibly competitive, especially if I were to consider long-term growth in my career. Ultimately my master's degree was a cop-out with a sister who had gone through the same route.

I think the overall effort to better provide nuance to the definition of homelessness, however, is in thinking of more creative solutions to help alleviate high rent prices in cities. Take, for instance, a charity that transformed a parking garage into a homeless shelter in Beddown, Australia, last December, by placing beds in a parking lot as a pop-up to see if it might help those without homes. In addition to the sleeping space, the charity provided services from doctors, nurses, dentists, hairdressers, and showers—all necessities that are hard to come by when struggling financially regardless of whether you are homeless or not. During their pop-up night, the charity had to turn down nine people due to overcapacity. However, as the idea proved to be successful, they are expected to partner with Secure Parking giving them access to six hundred more parking lots throughout Australia.

These charities are, no doubt, valuable, but they cannot solve the issue of homelessness alone. The issue of homelessness requires a holistic understanding of an individual who is struggling to survive with their limited and irregular wages. As the title suggests, "Maybe now more than ever, we can understand the fear that homeless people face," an article from *Real Change News* covers how the pandemic may be a reminder to some, or many families how delicate our livelihoods can be in the face of sudden national crisis. Other charities like Millionair Club Charity recognize that once a person experiences homelessness, it is difficult to escape the new reality. That is why their work—similar to the charity in Beddown providing services in addition to beds in their parking lots—provides "a hygiene center, laundry facility, job training workshops and uniforms (for no charge)...[while working] with partners to provide meals, a vision clinic and mobile medical and dental vans."

It is my hope that I can offer the same mindset to others, as we continue to navigate through a new market full of avant-garde consumers. Imagine a world where overhead costs are dramatically lower—people living inside electric vehicles with less furniture, less clothes, less stuff! Imagine a world where people are able to accept that, as we continue to work against climate change, we are also better equipped to deal with changing geographies by working nomadically in areas that provide us with the most sustainable livelihoods. This is the future that I began to imagine as I slept inside my van initially with my wardrobe as my blanket and pillow.

Much of our previous conceptions of housing are arguably limited due to learned helplessness, the idea that we do not attempt to remove ourselves from a negative situation because our experiences suggest that we are helpless and have no control over our destiny. It is in this thought process that I attempt to provide an alternative solution. Although the world has changed and is providing better alternatives, previous challenges in alternative housing options continue to challenge our approach to a new lifestyle.

Much of our approach to our lives are reinforced or discouraged through our experiences. Vanlife, while maybe discouraged by family or friends in the past, is now being encouraged by a new generation struggling to find housing. Vanlife has the ability to reinvent what it means to be successful in our new world. In changing the framework, people can learn to find joy and happiness in new ways—and maybe find more fulfillment in their lives than our parents ever did.

Imagine a world where, rather than being bound by geographies and financial limitations, you can continue to explore and cultivate your many passions in life, which can range from your career, love, and peace. When I wake up to nature's calling right outside my car door, I imagine a world where vanlife does not mean homelessness for any single American citizen but a stepping stone to fulfilling our destinies.

Imagine a world where, while our ancestors might want to rise up from their graves to disagree, we accept a nomadic lifestyle as a sign of stability rather than homelessness.

# PART 3

# FREEDOM AND LIBERTY FOR ALL!

CHAPTER FIVE

# Paving My Road

---

To no surprise, many friends—old and new—as well as strangers, acquaintances, colleagues, and many others, would often exclaim, "I have so many questions for you!" upon learning that I was pursuing "vanlife."

This chapter is dedicated to answering the most frequently asked questions I have encountered throughout my journey. I am grateful for the support and genuine curiosity among friends and strangers I have met along the way. The experience has been a way for me to connect with people intimately, covering more personal topics starting from accessing toilets to financing vanlife.

This chapter is intended to summarize and share my experiences and findings in the past year that I pursued vanlife. Some questions have pushed me to research beyond my need, to other alternative housing options. I hope that aspiring nomads (millennials, Gen Zers, or otherwise) will find the information interesting and helpful—perhaps opening them to new lifestyles and experiences.

## FRANKLIN'S VANLIFE FAQS

*TOILETS AND SHOWERS*

Not surprisingly, one of the most frequently asked questions among friends and strangers has been, "what do you do about the bathroom?"

The short answer is: a gym membership. A gym membership is often the best solution to daily showers and regular toilet access.

I have been fortunate in never having to pay for a gym membership. When I started, I had access to a free shower at my workplace. When I later changed jobs, I had access to a gym in my work building.

Access to a free shower, I realize, is a privilege that many people do not have. That said, it is a cost effective and important investment when pursuing vanlife, especially for those without a budget to buy an RV or to customize a compost toilet or otherwise within your van. It is worth mentioning that cleanliness is not only important for hygienic reasons but also to ensure that nomads are treated with respect from strangers or possible employers.

As I am giving this advice, however, I am critical of our reality. Today, with the growing rates of homelessness and the need for more public amenities, LA recently added more public toilets, as reported by the *LA Times* in 2017, although public amenities are known to be ineffective in maintaining services for those who expect to use the facilities at no cost. These bans came under the guise of helping the poor.

I've encountered various obstacles in accessing toilets and showers during my moves. I advocate for our nation to repeal laws outlawing pay toilets. As explained in the article, "Why Don't We Have Pay Toilets in America?" in *Pacific Standard* magazine, forty years ago, American states outlawed pay toilets, stating free access to toilets is a human right. Such policies, despite good intentions, prove discriminatory. Public facilities are often overused and left unusable.

Oftentimes, the next low-hanging fruits are cafes like Starbucks. Between my travels around New York City, Los Angeles, and Washington, DC, I have experienced a fight between a Starbucks employee and a homeless person frequenting the cafe bathrooms. Such experiences have convinced me that maintaining the current system is broken, leaving hardworking employees, law-abiding customers, and the struggling homeless people all unhappy.

As such, we need cheaper alternatives that reduce the use of free facilities. Consider sharing a couple bucks with a homeless person knowing that they can access a twenty-minute shower. Now consider letting a stranger into your home. While goodwill is always encouraged, we should consider the more practical methods of helping the masses. Bans on pay toilets are, ultimately barriers to affordable housing. People with unconventional homes can benefit from paying for hygienic and functional public facilities at cheap costs. Homeless people can also save up their small pocket change for occasional use of nicer facilities. Meanwhile, as the free facilities are used less, they are likely to require less maintenance and be of better condition. In my opinion, it is the practical way of keeping everyone happy.

To be clear, I am not advocating to eradicate free, public toilets. Simply, public policy can add cost-effective alternatives. Reducing the government and business burden by incorporating new models can help alleviate the burdens we share among individuals and the larger society.

In summary, we should create more sustainable options for public facilities. Less use of free, public toilets means that there will likely be less traffic and, therefore, be more accessible to those who need it most.

Adding pay toilets offers a new economy that might allow for further innovation that could change public access to sanitation and hygiene. Some businesses already have the concept of pay showers, which I learned as I visited rest stops during my road trip. Love's, for example, regularly provides timed shower rooms as a way for truckers to keep clean on the road. Expanding such amenities within urban pockets in which we can house nomads is likely to increase mobility for youth wishing to try and venture into city life.

### PARKING

When I serendipitously walked across the Grant Memorial in Riverside Park one afternoon after work, my colleague introduced me to a new neighborhood that had been right in front of my eyes. I simply never had the insight to take a closer look.

These hidden neighborhoods might be the oasis that people need to get back on their feet. Seeing the number of other RVs, smaller cars with shades, and even a rainbow-colored skoolie in the park helped me gain the courage to continue with my vanlife pursuit.

I know that I am not alone.

NBC Washington, for example, has reported that there is a small, invisible neighborhood on the edge of City College of San Francisco's main campus. Much like the safe haven I found in Upper West Manhattan, City College has created a below-the-radar community. I suspect that such safe havens are continuously at risk—challenged by neighborhood locals who find the "homeless" population disruptive. While I understand such concerns, it is my belief that such populations can be less disruptive and even synergistic to the local neighborhood with proper support.

To be clear, such discrimination, is not only immoral, but legally questionable. The US Supreme Court case *Papachristou v. City of Jacksonville* (1972) struck down Florida municipal law, suggesting that the homeless cannot be penalized for sleeping in public property when adequate shelter is not available elsewhere. However, in cities like Austin where homelessness rates are increasing, indecent exposure and loitering laws are increasing as a way to indirectly penalize those living in the streets. These laws have direct analogues in housing policy, where California's attempt to legalize accessory dwelling units proved ineffectual until municipalities were prevented from using other laws like parking requirements to ban the units. This is sad to me as I feel that more transparency between both sides can help everyone thrive.

For example, nonprofits like Safe Parking LA are helping alleviate the struggles among vanlivers and other people who are teetering between homelessness and temporary housing inside their vehicles. As shared in their website, within Los

Angeles County, there are over 15,700 people living inside their vehicles each night which accounts for more than one-third of the homeless population in the area.

The numbers prove that many people may be able to move forward with their lives with a bit more help. When Safe Parking LA opened its first lot in March 2018, they received 250 applications every 30 days, as the lots provided security to people who would otherwise live inside their vehicles with safety concerns and uncertainty of legal compliance. This is especially telling as there are similar lots in San Diego and Santa Barbara.

One of the luckiest parts of my early vanlife experience was that my safe haven was a five-minute walk from work. With four street cleanings throughout the week, I could take a quick lunch break to ensure that I parked my van from one side to another. In the chaos of NYC, I had a system that worked beautifully.

Things changed once I got a new job in Washington, DC. Without a safe haven parking lot I had to utilize both paid parking lots and special neighborhood parking permits. Not only were they expensive, but they were a hassle—often requiring me to make mistakes and pay fines before learning to park "responsibly." Amid all the changes, I have now transitioned beautifully into an apartment with my partner. That said, I hope that changes continue so that I may be on the road again in the future.

I trust our nation's ingenuity. The market is constantly producing creative solutions to growing societal problems. Commercializing safe parking lots throughout the nation that provide temperature control, in addition to safety and space, can change the dynamic of our nation.

## MAIL AND PERMANENT RESIDENCE

Simply put, pursuing vanlife full time is difficult without having a permanent residence address to register your driver's license.

A couple of months into my vanlife I transitioned from my job in NYC to a new position in DC without a permanent residence that I could use to update my driver's license. Eventually, a local parking police—noticing the same van parked in the general area for a couple of weeks—gave me a warning ticket lecturing me that I had to get a new driver's license within ninety days of the move. Of course, the catch-22 of the situation was that, in pursuing vanlife, a nomadic lifestyle contradicts the idea of a permanent residence.

As expected, getting a new license was challenging and expensive. Without a permanent residence in DC, I learned that other full-time nomads utilized UPS addresses. While the DMV would not accept PO boxes as permanent residence addresses, I learned that UPS advertised street addresses—mainly targeted for online businesses that did not require a physical store location.

Our current identification card system is antiquated. It is classist and socioeconomically unfair.

Feeling guilty after failing my road test the third time, I remember my parents having to pay for my second written exam. With only a few months left, I remember being pressured to get a driver's license to board a flight to Harvard. At the time, I had turned eighteen, and I could no longer board a flight with my student ID.

Nearly ten years later, I have new struggles as I can no longer rely on my parents' address to maintain my driver's license. We live in a nation where we utilize driver's licenses for most identification purposes. Yet, the price of upkeep is strenuous. Despite the fact that many Americans are living from paycheck to paycheck, our identity, homes, and job prospects are continuously at risk.

Basically, there is a clear divide between the have and have-nots. Our society seems to assume that we should have a permanent address, an identification card, and a job, when the reality is that these are very much out of reach for many people.

### WI-FI: FOUNDATIONS FOR THE NEW WORLD

In pursuing vanlife, the number one challenge, believe it or not, has been access to safe and stable Wi-Fi. With the added vulnerability from living inside a car, Wi-Fi provides knowledge at your fingertips, which is the extra level of protection for vanlivers.

*Where is a nearby gas station with a restroom open at 1 a.m.? If the parking area looks darker and more dangerous than it had looked a couple of hours prior, where else can I park? If my tire goes flat, how can I get it fixed?*

Being extra vulnerable, Wi-Fi is a key element for vanlivers in overcoming everyday obstacles. With the touch of your phone, Youtube or a quick Google search may help you relieve your bowels within the next ten minutes or make you feel a tad bit safer sleeping through the night.

This is all to say that, as opposed to traditional housing where things can often wait until the next day, vanlivers are pressured to act quickly. This is true for all vulnerable populations. Americans living paycheck to paycheck are likely to hoard food or toilet paper when prices spike and their livelihoods are threatened.

Unfortunately, the world's most vulnerable citizens do not have access to Wi-Fi. The pandemic has highlighted the social inequity in our nation—let alone the globe— and arguably the biggest social injustice has been the inability to connect via the internet.

Today, the internet is important for all ranges of work, especially with the growing need of online access since the COVID-19 outbreak. Therefore, expanding broadband access, the increasingly popular form of internet connection due to its speed, is vital. Last April, the Pew Research Center found that "87 percent of adults [said] that the internet has been at least important for them personally during the coronavirus outbreak, including 53 percent who [described] it as essential."

However, expanding broadband access must come in parallel with securing public wireless networks seeing that, during COVID-19, "roughly half of Americans with lower incomes [reported being] worried about paying their broadband and cell phone bills over the coming months."

More than eighteen million Americans, many in rural areas, lack high quality, affordable broadband service—none more so than those pursuing vanlife. This is unsustainable. American broadband networks like AT&T and Verizon have found the gaps in providing reliable Wi-Fi networks to low-income families and Americans in nontraditional housing in underserved areas.

Thankfully, technology is not only becoming more available but also becoming a source of income. Two decades ago, Youtube and Instagram did not exist. Today, a number of people create a living as content creators and influencers.

With the 2008 recession, I remember our family struggling to make ends meet. My mother, who had supplemented my father's work at home, officially got on payroll as a part-time employee. The concept of commerce has also changed toward more personalized marketing, focusing on the individual and marketing yourself online. With more online marketplaces, many stores are losing their physical retail locations and are instead focusing on their online sales.

Vanlife challenged my preconceived notions of stability and living well. Today, as I have a job that I could work remotely, I am continuously paving a road in which I can live off the road. While I have stabilized myself back into a comfortable apartment, I am only too aware of the advantages of being able to tap into the virtual world.

A vanliver has an unprecedented advantage in the new world full of technology and growing access to Wi-Fi. Time will tell if nomads will be able to construct a world that continuously innovates toward a freer and happier future.

## EXPLORING OTHER ALTERNATIVE HOUSING OPTIONS
While vanlife was optimal for my situation—considering that I wanted stealth, cost-effectiveness, and convenience—I realized that there were a number of options that might fit for different environments.

### VANLIFE, RVS & TRAILERS
Considering that RVs and trailers have been frequented throughout history, as far as Mongolian nomads to the Oregon Trail, vanlife is not a novel concept. Whether it came in the form of herding cattle with horses or riding carriages, our ancestors had a history of constant migration.

What is special about vanlife, however, is the notion that with the technological advancement of cars, vehicle spaces initially intended for the use of driving only are often customized (ranging from singles, couples, to a small family unit). To me, the fact that vanlife starts from cars intended for driving only represents a human adaptation to the environment rather than vice versa.

Unlike RVs and trailers, which favor living conditions over mobility, vanlife oftentimes favors mobility over living conditions. Furthermore, vanlife suggests a level of customization that adheres more closely to one's resources and tastes—making the entire experience more individual and identity based. Take, for instance, *Expedition Happiness*, a film following the journey of a couple from Europe traveling through the Americas, showing the emotional and psychological attachments involved in mobile living.

Much of the book covers my vanlife. As such, I will cover skoolies, houseboats, and tiny homes in this section. Additionally, I will discuss Airbnbs as they are helpful tools to pursue alternative housing options strategically.

### SKOOLIES

One of the most exciting alternative housing options may very well be a skoolie.

What is a skoolie?

A skoolie is a school bus that has been converted into a living space. As Tobias Robert, a writer for RISE (a sustainable home improvement product company), puts it, skoolie is the "original tiny home." As school buses are typically larger than vans, they provide more comfort, space, and options.

While parking in Riverside Park in NYC, I saw a couple of skoolies on the block, with my favorite being the rainbow skoolie painted in exciting colors. What was especially appealing about the idea was that a skoolie could potentially be larger than an average apartment in Manhattan.

However, being conspicuous has its consequences. I remember walking back to the van one afternoon and noticing that one of the bus windows was broken. To this day, I am not sure what happened, but it is important to note the added vulnerabilities in living inside a public space as opposed to private property.

That said, if safety and space is guaranteed, I believe that a skoolie is, in fact, the best mobile home choice.

Before purchasing my van, I sought out external advice from other vanlivers. One ex-vanliver, excited about my project, offered his skoolie to get me started.

Take my word that I was tempted. I thought over the offer for days and weeks. Ultimately, I had to decline.

Skoolies are, no doubt, awesome! But, for a young professional who wants to focus on starting his career, I had to save my dream skoolie for another day.

### HOUSEBOATS ON MARINAS

As the name suggests, houseboats are boats that are used as houses. Houseboats are essentially RVs on water. For those who want to live in a more idyllic setting cheaply, living in a marina in a houseboat can be a great choice.

One ex-vanliver I chatted with strongly advocated that I live in a marina. Having lived inside a van himself, he had felt exhausted. He explained that he constantly felt judged by others.

The problem, for me, was that a boat would not provide me with the same mobility and practicality as a van. Living inside a boat requires a body of water, which immediately limited my geography. Furthermore, as living inside a marina is more permanent than a van, it would be helpful to ask additional questions before taking the leap. Starting from fueling the boat, to power, water, and Wi-Fi, houseboats will likely require a bit more planning beforehand.

Living inside a van meant that I could drive to a McDonald's first thing in the morning for a quick McGriddle and coffee as well as use their public bathroom.

The discussion was, nonetheless, fruitful, as I decided upon a commercial-looking Mercedes Benz Sprinter van as a way to camouflage myself within the city.

It proved effective. Those who eventually found out that I was living inside my van would share that they would have never imagined that somebody was living inside it. The anonymity helped me feel safer.

At the same time, marinas have a fundamentally different lifestyle. For those who have the time and money, marinas can be a safe haven that provide an incredible luxury at the fraction of the cost. One article from Neighbor.com, a storage listing website, suggests that a houseboat is significantly cheaper than a traditional house, as the average annual cost only amounts to $6,000.

I can definitely see its appeal and hope that more options become available in the future.

### TINY HOMES

Fascination with tiny homes has been a big part of my vanlife journey. It was embarrassing, at first, to share that I had never watched *Tiny House Nation*, available on Netflix and A&E.

Now, having watched seasons of the show and becoming heavily addicted to the concept, I understand the appeal. Tiny homes seem like the smart choice—a budget-friendly, eco-friendly, and picturesque option.

Having pursued vanlife, however, I am not surprised to hear that the reality of van and tiny homes in general is that they are not as glamorous as is depicted on television shows and social media. Starting without a clear idea of the challenges and difficulty can lead individuals to abandon their homes.

Just like most anything, tiny homes provide advantages and disadvantages.

My take on tiny homes is that an individual should not leap into the prospect that it will provide a traditional house experience. To be realistic, one should recognize how to moderate the expected challenges, sometimes utilizing their privileges to supplement the pitfalls.

For example, when I first read about vanlife, I learned that many workers in Silicon Valley decided to live inside their cars to sleep because they would spend most of their time in the office anyway. As a young professional in NYC, I thought I could emulate a similar model.

The plunge allowed me a five-minute walk to work, plenty of amenities open 24/7 nearby, and beautiful scenery right outside my vehicle.

However, I struggled with the heat and cold throughout the seasons. I cracked the screen of my new phone in the dark one night because the van was so dark and cold. I had to obsessively plan my day around street parking, which could distract from the important tasks at work. In short, my vanlife experience had its drawbacks.

Tiny homes, while cheaper, do not guarantee a great location to commute easily to work. They also, no doubt, have various inconveniences in the form of everyday chores or projects at home. Despite these challenges, it is important to see your circumstances for what they are before you get discouraged. After all, when done correctly, big risks come with big rewards.

### AIRBNB

Between purchasing my van and renovating the vehicle to live inside it, I lived in Airbnbs. I believe that Airbnbs can be an effective tool to ease into vanlife for beginners.

When I first took the plunge and bought my van, I had no idea where to start. All I knew was that I felt vulnerable living inside an expensive NYC apartment. I felt uncomfortable knowing that my parents knew my address. I found strength in mobility, being able to move my life at any time.

Luckily, I already had some experience utilizing Airbnbs to ease into a new city. After graduate school, I first moved into Airbnbs at a cheap monthly rate so that I could spend some time exploring the different neighborhoods and thinking about where would be my best fit.

Similarly, as I figured out the logistics for the van, I moved from one Airbnb to another between neighborhoods that I was curious to explore. Rather than Bushwick, I got to walk around Upper Manhattan.

Airbnb can have various reputations—mostly that it is for a couple nights' stay for travel. Many people I have conversed with were surprised to hear that Airbnb often created monthly discounts so that their prices were competitive to leases or subleases.

I find the experience contrary. Airbnbs, with their cheap monthly rates, provide a convenient way to ease into a neighborhood. Due to their visibility, I felt that I knew what I was signing up for. I felt safe with my choices and thought the prices were fair. In addition to the convenience of the platform, knowing that the payment methods are secure and that the listings are regularly monitored for safety makes it especially appealing.

Similarly, if vanlife and mobile living continue to boom, I wonder if Airbnb can open a subset for Carbnbs in which people list spaces to park vehicles. I believe that such a market may emerge as urban prices continue to surge. In my mind, there is a distinctive opportunity for people who have the ability and capacity to accommodate mobile-living visitors, as they are likely to pay for additional services like access to toilets and shower, parking and safety, and Wi-Fi.

**TAKING THE LEAP**
Discussing vanlife, while exciting and intriguing, is challenging because it is a highly individual and custom experience. Similar alternative housing options like tiny homes,

houseboats, and skoolies are all interesting for the same reason—the thought that they may be a more personal fit that will enhance our lives.

My yearlong experience of pursuing vanlife confirms this thought. However, I do not want to disillusion readers that the experience will solve all your problems or that it will always be worth the trouble. In fact, the plunge will likely add more problems to your journey as much as it provides its amazing perks.

Vanlife, in the context of our constantly migrating ancestors, is not a truly novel concept. As such, it is simply another lifestyle that may help us transition into a better world. I can see how some may see vanlife as original, but others might consider it a relabel for past concepts. Some see vanlife as a form of glorified homelessness, while others see a smart housing option.

Ultimately, as in the case of most real-life issues, understanding context is important in making wise decisions. One of the most valuable lessons I learned while pursuing vanlife was about self-acceptance. I feared my judgment because my parents disapproved. I feared that my decisions would lead to dire consequences and that I had to accept my status quo.

While I did end up with many of the challenges that I expected beforehand, I now know that the experience was fully worth it. Along the ride, I found freedom, love, and confidence. Even knowing that there is the chance of a car accident, driving behind the steering wheel is still exhilarating. It is very much worth the trouble.

For those of you who are as risk averse as I am, I hope that you will continue to keep an open mind to new experiences and opportunities. Like many others, I thought that wisdom comes with age. Nope, wisdom comes from experience. While time is on our side, it does not guarantee a mastery of knowledge and requires our most active participation. When the time comes, you know that you can hit the open road with no regrets.

## CHAPTER SIX

# Bon Voyage!

---

Every story is unique.

While the notion that we are all special may come off as a cliché, considering the probability for each individual to exist in a moment at a time and place is, in fact, miraculous.

Believing in this miracle, I decided to share my vanlife experience. A simple Google or Youtube search will find you countless articles, videos, and classes to build out a van of your own.

What would make my book, my narrative, unique?

I was in desperate search for an answer, as the book was a means to an end in which I needed to get the support and resources to maintain an adventurous and rather risky venture.

I am so thankful to the many people who have encouraged me to pursue my passion project. Having gone through vanlife for an entire year full time, I realize that vanlife is an opportunity. To me, it was a starter home and an interim temporary shelter that reduced some of the headaches that come with changing jobs, moving from city to city, and generally portioning out my paycheck to make sure that (other than rent) I can start chipping away at my student loans.

In the same way that property became a symbol of independence and freedom to many Americans in the early days, vanlife is an opportunity to reinvent the world in a way that promotes ownership to drive our own lives. If this book has any value to offer, it is my hope that it might give my readers courage. To those who are struggling, it may be reassuring to know that a Harvard graduate can be struggling as much as a recent GED graduate. In the modern world, we are all struggling. We are all on an equal playing field.

I still remember my first time driving on the highway—the first time I visited a car dealer in anticipation of buying a car. Now, as I expertly follow the directions on Google Maps, I reflect back on my journey.

**CHAPTER REFLECTION**
I started my first chapter with "Coming Out" to share how my vanlife journey began and to convey that "it takes a village to raise a child."

My LGBTQ+ experience is integral to my Harvard to homeless narrative. I consider myself fortunate in having the opportunity to attend Harvard and to eventually have the resources to pursue vanlife. It was not an easy journey, and I assume that either experience would be challenging for many others as well.

Not everyone has the option to come out—whether it be your sexual orientation or in pursuing your own passion, career, or major.

A big part of this struggle is financial independence. Younger people do not have financial independence mainly because of housing, which was not the case decades back.

My second chapter, "Love in the Time of Corona," caused me much pain and joy, as I got to share how vanlife helped me find love (amid a worldwide pandemic). My partner Patrick's experience is also valuable to the discussion around homelessness, as he found himself homeless in Los Angeles for over five years. Vanlife shows there are new options for people who are undergoing the many struggles that Patrick went through himself.

I wrote the third chapter, "The H-Bomb," while following the typical American narrative, of a "rags-to-riches" story (an Asian American boy with immigrant parents from South Korea with essentially nothing eventually makes his way to Harvard). This chapter also discusses the aftermath and the realities that may be hiding behind the feel-good fantasy. In this regard, vanlife shows how my underdog story continued after my acceptance to Harvard, as I continued to fear homelessness and failure.

Additionally, "The "H-Bomb" discusses the issue of identity by discussing the concept of "humble bragging," "trauma porn," and traditions. These are all important issues in a world where social media often highlights and, therefore, exaggerates life successes. Facebook and Instagram feeds oftentimes show our best moments rather than the times we are anxious, broken, or lonely; although, as the chapter discusses, the opposite extreme also rings true for audiences.

In a time where the public is so connected and hypersensitive to our virtual persona, how can we discover our identity and share it with the world? More importantly, can we retain the many joys associated with sharing our life stories and experiences with the world?

The fourth chapter digs deeper into, "Defining Homelessness." Defining and honing in on categories is a human pursuit. It is also utilitarian.

For policymakers, it is important to define categories of "homelessness" or "alternative housing" as a way to produce appropriate services, regulations, and guidelines for the associated communities.

To some, defining terms that are associated with certain connotations helps us better understand the narrative. By providing nuance to words, our communities can better empathize with others. In understanding that homelessness can always be an upcoming reality for anyone (regardless of your academic pedigree or wealth), we can act with more compassion and purpose.

Lastly, before concluding my book here, the final chapter, "Paving My Road," is intended for those who are interested in trying vanlife for themselves or curious about the frequently asked questions that I collected during my journey.

While every interaction with friends and strangers is unique, certain patterns emerged during our conversations. Knowing that there are common questions and topics of interest, I have attempted to organize them neatly into one chapter for quick and easy review.

As I reflect and summarize each chapter here, it is my hope that my book may be a helpful reference for readers.

That said, I would like to start concluding my journey by digging a bit deeper into how my vanlife started from the points I made in my prior chapters.

**MY FIRST BOOK: *THE ART OF NAPPING***
Putting oneself out in the world, wide open to judgment, is hard.

Like others, there are many fears associated with putting yourself out there. In the same way that some of us get butterflies in our stomachs when we go up on stage to perform, putting out any piece of writing for others to read and judge is usually more anxiety inducing than calming.

Still, our hopes and sense of excitement can give us the courage to take the plunge. Thinking that it may be the only time and opportunity in which I may be able to write a book, I wrote about a topic that I believed to be interesting: sleep.

Having gone through both Harvard and Georgetown, I wrote *The Art of Napping: The Sleeping Samurai and the Dormant Dragon* with much pressure and hope in 2017. Thinking back and taking the time to reflect, I believe that ignorance was a blessing in disguise.

The chance that I took then helped me reflect about my curiosity, passion, and identity. Starting from my interest in nap pods that originated in Japan, my research led me to topics that ignited my fire. As I was struggling to hit my manuscript deadline, I still remember covering an article from *RT* reporting a woman who died inside her car in 2014 while sleeping between her shifts. The story of naps, while it had its entertainment value as a pleasant and intriguing concept, was not frivolous. The issue was a matter of social inequality and urban hardship.

As I started thinking about smaller living spaces, I warmed up to the idea of living inside a van. More importantly, as I learned to share my writing and take in feedback constructively (and hopefully gracefully), I was able to entertain the idea of writing *From Harvard to Homeless*. Writing this book has been a cathartic experience, as the nature of the topic required me to discuss my personal experiences in detail and share my most raw and honest reflections.

## I AM ENOUGH

To me, the issue of injustice is important because it helps me recognize my circumstances more clearly and help pave a better way for myself as well as others. I genuinely believe that knowledge is power; there is power in being able to enunciate your position in the context of larger society. The issue of social injustice in affordable housing can really impact anyone, and at times, the thought is frightening and harsh.

At the time when I was writing my book, I was told by my publishers to think big, think the impossible. The idea that I had settled on was virtual reality rooms. As I struggled to find the resources to fund a start-up of an idea that I had no foundation to start on, I continuously attempted to connect my reality with my fantasy. Today, in navigating through my mistakes and insecurities, I have found a way to connect my interest and passion in a practical way.

Today, I find my decisions and long-term vision meaningful and fulfilling. It was a long journey to get to this point, and I am aware that there is still a long way to go—not just for me but for those who may want to join me along the road. Personally, the most exciting part of my book project is that my adventures extend beyond my personal experiences to the needs and desires of the wider society, which feels like an extension of my undergraduate studies in anthropology: "the science which tells us that people are the same the whole world over—except when they are different," as quoted by Nancy Banks-Smith, a British television and radio critic.

My hope is that I will be able to utilize my good luck to spread it toward others—for good karma, of course. I started my vanlife out of need but found a deep appreciation for my project. I think many others are not as fortunate. Some people may state that everyone is capable of finding their passion, but I disagree slightly. I think that everyone is capable of finding their passion if they are under the right environment. In today's world where people are becoming more aware of how to eloquently describe social injustices and realities, I feel that cliché advice of the past (such as, "follow your passion") have become more nuanced (like, "don't quit your job to pursue your passion"). From my experience, it is more vital to be vigilant of the world you are living in and think about how to progress in small steps. As you move forward, you may realize that you are walking a road toward your life passion.

Every morning, after walking from my van to the office, showering, and making myself a cup of coffee, I would read through the news and browse through my social media feeds to see if there were any readings that might interest me. One serendipitous day, I ran across a LinkedIn post that distinguished curiosity over passion. As you are reading through this book, you may actually notice that I reference the concept continuously throughout the book.

I believe that the genius in the concept they describe is that people need to be allowed to follow their curiosities if they are to eventually find a passion. Without the ability to take risks, try out new experiences, and interact with new ideas, peoples, and concepts, there is unlikely to be a life passion or anything to continue building and developing it. The article I read back at Harvard was the external stimulus that intrigued me and piqued my curiosity. Over the years, my curiosity developed as I researched about nap pods, sleep deprivation, and social injustices in our world and workplace. It is my hope that others will be able to explore their curiosities in the way that I had. However, to get there, I feel that there is still much to be done.

Today, there is much reason to be hopeful; people are able to access new ideas, new perspectives, online. People have access to cheap material goods including a smartphone that democratizes technology like never before. While these developments have not perfected our world yet, seeing all the ruptures and social discomforts of 2020, all of these struggles may be growing pains. The journey continues. Bon voyage!

# Acknowledgements

―――

My vanlife journey from conception, execution, and reflection could not have been possible without the many generous and understanding souls out in this universe.

Paula Harker, Peter Glebo, and Nina Lombardi were the foundation, the rock, to build my project. They listened to my ideas without judgment, and I felt like I could share my most intimate and personal details without fear.

Next, I would like to give the biggest thanks to Bespoke of Winchester for providing all the resources and support I needed to execute my project. I would not have been able to successfully pursue vanlife and publish this book without all of you: Tony, Nino, Christian & Rolando, Jack & Doug, and Sergio. Thank you all for helping me build my comfortable and beautiful safe haven.

I would like to thank George Ciobanu for being so generous to house me when the pandemic started. To have a sanctuary during that time was so valuable because I was rethinking the direction of my journey, as I was making fundamental life changes.

I would like to also thank Lingbo Jiang for putting faith into my journey long before it started.

Thank you to Iuval, David, Emily, Anne, and Clint for sharing their alternative housing experiences during my early stages of my research on vanlife.

Lastly, I would like to thank the incredibly understanding team at the Creator Institute. Morgan Rohde, I felt that I could always turn to you for my manuscript edits without judgment. You are an angel! Your emotional and moral support were invaluable. Linda Berardelli, thank you for your continued patience and accommodation. Your faith in me helped me cross the finish line!

I am thankful to everyone else who has helped put my story out in the universe. I have worked hard to keep my story raw, because I owe honesty to the community that has helped build me into who I am today. This is not the end; it is just the beginning.

Bon Voyage!

# Appendix

---

**INTRODUCTION**

- ABC News Center 7, "From Yale to the streets of Los Angeles - homeless man presents his life's story as a warning." *ABC News Center 7,* press release September 17, 2019.

- ABC News Center 7, "Yale grad gets help from fellow alum after living on streets of LA for years." *ABC News Center 7,* November 9, 2019.

- Bersin, Josh. "Why Aren't Wages Keeping Up? It's Not The Economy, It's Management." *Forbes,* October 31, 2018.

- Chu, Melissa. "The Man, The Boy, and The Donkey: A Lesson on Critics." *Medium,* September 24, 2018.

- Collins, Andrew. "Living in Cars Is Becoming Even More of a Thing in Los Angeles." *Jalopnik,* July 18, 2019.

- Funk, Cary, Alec Tyson. "Partisan Differences Over the Pandemic Response Are Growing." *Pew Research Center,* June 3, 2020.

- Holder, Sarah, "Finding Home in a Parking Lot." *CityLab,* February 11, 2019.

- Leonhardt, Megan. "EARN Millennials earn 20% less than baby boomers did—despite being better educated."

- *CNBC,* November 5, 2019.

- Passy, Jacob. "Millennials spend a staggering amount on rent by the time they're 30." *MarketWatch,* March 26, 2018.

- *True Colors United*, "LGBTQ Youth are 120% More Likely to Experience Homelessness." 2021.

- Youtube. "Jennelle Eliana." *Jennelle Eliana Vanlife,* last modified on April 29, 2021.

- Youtube. "Katie Carney." *Katie Carney Vanlife,* last modified on October 29, 2021.

## CHAPTER 1

- *ABC News Center 7,* "From Yale to the streets of Los Angeles - homeless man presents his life's story as a warning." September 17, 2019.

- Bialik, Kristen. "Millennial life: How young adulthood today compares with prior generations." *Pew Research Center,* February 14, 2019.

- Hull, Megan. "How Homelessness Drives LGBTQ+ Addiction." *The Recovery Village,* February 24, 2020.

- Invisible People. "About Invisible People." Introduction, 2008-2021.

- Kristof, Nicholas. "3 TVs and No Food: Growing Up Poor in America." *The New York Times,* October 29, 2016.

- Long, Heather. "The coronavirus economy is exposing how easy it is to fall from the middle class into poverty." *The Washington Post,* May 8, 2020.

- Moore, Melissa. "40% of Homeless Youth Are LGBTQ – What We Can Do." TedXTalks, May 7, 2019.

- Morton, M.H., Dworsky, A., & Samuels, G.M. "Missed opportunities: Youth homelessness in America." *Chapin Hall at the University of Chicago,* 2017.

- Powers, Ashley. "The College Try." *California Sunday Magazine,* September 20, 2017.

- *Preble Street.* "Myths about the homeless" April 4, 2011.

- Urbina, Ian "Keeping It Secret as the Family Car Becomes a Home" *The New York Times,* April 2, 2006.

## CHAPTER 2

- Ausubel, Jacob. "Older people are more likely to live alone in the U.S. than elsewhere in the world." *Pew Research Center,* March 10, 2020.

- Barroso, Amanda, Kim Parker, Jesse Bennet. "As Millennials Near 40, They're Approaching Family Life Differently Than Previous Generations." *Pew Research Center,* May 27, 2020.

- Centers of Disease Control and Prevention. "2014 Surgeon General's Report: The Health Consequences of Smoking—50 Years of Progress" last reviewed in 2014.

- Centers of Disease Control and Prevention. "Tobacco Use by Geographic Region" last reviewed November 25, 2019.

- Cray, Kate. "They Met During Lockdown. They Realized Who They Were Dating Later." *The Atlantic,* August 9, 2021.

- Noonan, Rita. "Rural America in Crisis: The Changing Opioid Overdose Epidemic." *Public Health Matter Blog,* November 28, 2017.

- Pew Research Center. "The Virtues and Downsides of Online Dating" Internet and Research. Accessed on February 6, 2020.

- Shapiro, Joseph. "How Driver's License Suspensions Unfairly Target The Poor" *NPR,* January 5, 2015.

- Shipley, Ahlishia, "Opioid Crisis Affects All Americans, Rural and Urban" U.S. Department of Agriculture, August 3, 2021.

## CHAPTER 3

- Baker, Billy. "Not easy for Harvard grads to say they went there." *The Boston Globe,* May 28, 2012.

- *Doug in a Pub.* "Big T & Little t" Blog published on December 4, 2020.

- Fandos, Nicholas. "Harvard Sophomore Charged in Bomb Threat." *The Harvard Crimson,* Last updated on December 17, 2013.

- Friedman, Amy, Justin Worland. "Weld Visitor Abe Liu: I Was Lonely" *The Harvard Crimson,* December 14, 2011.

- Gaertner, Andrew. "My White Bubble Protected Me Against Critical Race Theory, Until Now." *Medium,* August 7.

- *Harvard Political Review.* "We're All Eldo Kim" Published on December 18, 2013.

- *Harvard Political Review.* "We're Not All Eldo Kim" Published on December 18, 2013.

- Hava, Guillermo. " Death on the Charles." *The Harvard Crimson,* September 16, 2020.

- Richards, Hunter. "Impractical Traditions." *Harvard Independent,* September 13, 2016.

- Sweet, Jacob. "How Harvard Profited On Keeping Time." *Harvard Magazine,* September-October 2021.

## CHAPTER 4

- BackCountry Chronicle. "Wilderness Survival Rules of 3 – Air, Shelter, Water and Food" 2011-2021.

- Banerjee, Mohini. "'Poverty Impedes Cognitive Function' – Reason to Help, or Blame, the Poor?" The Hastings Center, September 26, 2013.

- Demichele, Thomas. "Being Gay Used to Be Illegal." *Fact/Myth,* August 27, 2016.

- Gold, Michael. "They Came to N.Y.C. for Acceptance. Now They Need Jobs." *The New York Times,* April 20, 2021.

- Legal Information Institute. "42 U.S. Code § 11302 – General definition of homeless individual" revised on July 22, 2014.

- Bahney, Anna. "Minimum wage workers can't afford rent anywhere in America." *CNN,* July 15, 2021

- National Alliance to End Homelessness. "Changes in the HUD Definition of 'Homeless'" published on January 18, 2012.

- O'Connell, Patrick. "Maybe now more than ever, we can understand the fear that homeless people face." Real Change, April 8, 2020.

- Pygas, Mark. "Charity transforms parking garages into homeless shelters at night." *Megaphone,* November 15, 2019.

- Spencer, Kyle. "In College and Homeless." *The New York Times,* February 20, 2020.

- *Stack Exchange.* "Do I need a physical address to get a driver's license?" edited February 1, 2016.

- *Vanholio.* "Is Living in Your Van Illegal?" Updated on January 26, 2018.

- Wareham, Jamie. "Map Shows Where It's Illegal To Be Gay – 30 Years Since WHO Declassified Homosexuality As Disease." *Forbes Magazine,* May 17, 2020.

## CHAPTER 5

- AETV. "Tiny House Nation" A&E TV.

- Gordon, Aaron. "WHY DON'T WE HAVE PAY TOILETS IN AMERICA?" Pacific Standard, June 14, 2017.

- Holland, Gale. "L.A. adds more public toilets as homeless crisis grows." Los Angeles Times, February 21, 2020.

- House, Sophie. "Pay Toilets Are Illegal in Much of the U.S. They Shouldn't Be." Bloomberg CityLab, November 19, 2018.

- Humphries, Monica. "These Parking Lots Give Homeless People a Safe Place to Sleep for the Night." Nation Swell, March 26, 2019.

- National Alliance to End Homelessness. "Exploring the Crisis of Unsheltered Homelessness" NAEH, June 20, 2018.

- Neighbor. "15 Questions You Should Ask Before Buying a Houseboat." April 5, 2020.

- Roberts, Tobias. "What is a Skoolie? A Complete Guide." RISE, May 26, 2019.

- SafeParkingLA. "Nobody Plans to Be Homeless." 2018-2019.

- Wells, Caleigh. "LA County Opens Another Parking Lot For Homeless People To Sleep Safely In Their Cars." LA List, January 9, 2019.

- Willet-Wei, Megan. "Living in tiny homes was much harder than these people realized." Insider, July 27, 2015 https://www.businessinsider.com/five-people-who-abandoned-their-tiny-homes-2015-7.

## CHAPTER 6

- Banks-Smith. "Anthropology is the science which tells us that people are the same the whole world over-except when they are different." *AZ Quotes.*

- Gilbert, Elizabeth. "Choosing Curiosity Over Fear." *On Being,* May 24, 2018.

- Quibuyen, Janelle. "Whatever you do, don't quit your job to pursue your passion." *Quartz,* June 7, 2016.

- RT. "Woman working 4 jobs to make ends meet dies while napping in car between shifts." *USA News,* August 29, 2014.

Printed by Libri Plureos GmbH in Hamburg, Germany